Obesity

Opposing Viewpoints®

DATE DUE

NOV 01 2013			
APR 12 2014			
NOV 18 2019			

Obesity

Opposing Viewpoints®

Other Books of Related Interest

Obesity

Opposing Viewpoints®

Andrea C. Nakaya, *Book Editor*

Bruce Glassman, *Vice President*
Bonnie Szumski, *Publisher*
Helen Cothran, *Managing Editor*

OPPOSING
VIEWPOINTS®
SERIES

GREENHAVEN PRESS
An imprint of Thomson Gale, a part of The Thomson Corporation

THOMSON
™
GALE

Detroit • New York • San Francisco • San Diego • New Haven, Conn.
Waterville, Maine • London • Munich

LIBRARY OF CONGRESS CATALOGING-IN-PUBLICATION DATA

Obesity : opposing viewpoints / Andrea C. Nakaya, book editor.
   p. cm. — (Opposing viewpoints series)
Includes bibliographical references and index.
ISBN 0-7377-3233-4 (lib. : alk. paper) — ISBN 0-7377-3234-2 (pbk. : alk. paper)
   1. Obesity—Popular works. I. Nakaya, Andrea C., 1976– . II. Opposing viewpoints series (Unnumbered)
RC628.O289 2006
616.3'98—dc22   2005040333

Printed in the United States of America

Contents

Why Consider Opposing Viewpoints?

"The only way in which a human being can make some approach to knowing the whole of a subject is by hearing what can be said about it by persons of every variety of opinion and studying all modes in which it can be looked at by every character of mind. No wise man ever acquired his wisdom in any mode but this."

John Stuart Mill

In our media-intensive culture it is not difficult to find differing opinions. Thousands of newspapers and magazines and dozens of radio and television talk shows resound with differing points of view. The difficulty lies in deciding which opinion to agree with and which "experts" seem the most credible. The more inundated we become with differing opinions and claims, the more essential it is to hone critical reading and thinking skills to evaluate these ideas. Opposing Viewpoints books address this problem directly by presenting stimulating debates that can be used to enhance and teach these skills. The varied opinions contained in each book examine many different aspects of a single issue. While examining these conveniently edited opposing views, readers can develop critical thinking skills such as the ability to compare and contrast authors' credibility, facts, argumentation styles, use of persuasive techniques, and other stylistic tools. In short, the Opposing Viewpoints Series is an ideal way to attain the higher-level thinking and reading skills so essential in a culture of diverse and contradictory opinions.

In addition to providing a tool for critical thinking, Opposing Viewpoints books challenge readers to question their own strongly held opinions and assumptions. Most people form their opinions on the basis of upbringing, peer pressure, and personal, cultural, or professional bias. By reading carefully balanced opposing views, readers must directly confront new ideas as well as the opinions of those with whom they disagree. This is not to simplistically argue that everyone who reads opposing views will—or should—change his or her opinion. Instead, the series enhances readers' understanding of their own views by encouraging confrontation with opposing ideas. Careful examination of others' views can lead to the readers' understanding of the logical inconsistencies in their own opinions, perspective on why they hold an opinion, and the consideration of the possibility that their opinion requires further evaluation.

Evaluating Other Opinions

To ensure that this type of examination occurs, Opposing Viewpoints books present all types of opinions. Prominent spokespeople on different sides of each issue as well as well-known professionals from many disciplines challenge the reader. An additional goal of the series is to provide a forum for other, less known, or even unpopular viewpoints. The opinion of an ordinary person who has had to make the decision to cut off life support from a terminally ill relative, for example, may be just as valuable and provide just as much insight as a medical ethicist's professional opinion. The editors have two additional purposes in including these less known views. One, the editors encourage readers to respect others' opinions—even when not enhanced by professional credibility. It is only by reading or listening to and objectively evaluating others' ideas that one can determine whether they are worthy of consideration. Two, the inclusion of such viewpoints encourages the important critical thinking skill of objectively evaluating an author's credentials and bias. This evaluation will illuminate an author's reasons for taking a particular stance on an issue and will aid in readers' evaluation of the author's ideas.

It is our hope that these books will give readers a deeper understanding of the issues debated and an appreciation of the complexity of even seemingly simple issues when good and honest people disagree. This awareness is particularly important in a democratic society such as ours in which people enter into public debate to determine the common good. Those with whom one disagrees should not be regarded as enemies but rather as people whose views deserve careful examination and may shed light on one's own.

Thomas Jefferson once said that "difference of opinion leads to inquiry, and inquiry to truth." Jefferson, a broadly educated man, argued that "if a nation expects to be ignorant and free . . . it expects what never was and never will be." As individuals and as a nation, it is imperative that we consider the opinions of others and examine them with skill and discernment. The Opposing Viewpoints Series is intended to help readers achieve this goal.

David L. Bender and Bruno Leone,
Founders

Greenhaven Press anthologies primarily consist of previously published material taken from a variety of sources, including periodicals, books, scholarly journals, newspapers, government documents, and position papers from private and public organizations. These original sources are often edited for length and to ensure their accessibility for a young adult audience. The anthology editors also change the original titles of these works in order to clearly present the main thesis of each viewpoint and to explicitly indicate the opinion presented in the viewpoint. These alterations are made in consideration of both the reading and comprehension levels of a young adult audience. Every effort is made to ensure that Greenhaven Press accurately reflects the original intent of the authors included in this anthology.

Introduction

"McDonald's food can fit into a healthy, well-balanced diet based upon the choice and variety available on our menu."

—Lisa Howard, McDonald's spokeswoman

"It seems that wherever America's fast food chains go, waistlines start expanding."

—Eric Schlosser, author of Fast Food Nation

In 2002 filmmaker Morgan Spurlock was watching television when a particular news story caught his attention: Two girls in New York were suing McDonald's because, they claimed, the food had made them overweight. A representative for the fast food chain contended that its food could not be linked to the girls' obesity and was, in fact, healthy and nutritious. Spurlock doubted the truth of the McDonald's spokesperson, and set out to prove his case. "If it's that good for me, then I should be able to eat it for breakfast, lunch, and dinner for 30 days straight with no side effects, right?" he theorized. The result was his 2004 documentary, *Super Size Me*, in which he embarked on a thirty-day diet consisting exclusively of McDonald's food. At the end of thirty days, Spurlock concluded that McDonald's food was far from healthy and nutritious: He had gained twenty-five pounds and was suffering from a number of serious, obesity-related health problems.

Spurlock's film is only one example of how, as worldwide obesity rates have skyrocketed, McDonald's has been widely blamed as one of the causes. In view of the statistics, it is not surprising that many people have made a connection between obesity rates and McDonald's, one of the largest fast food chains in the world. America leads the world in obesity rates, with two-thirds of its population classified as obese; at the same time, one in four Americans eats at a fast food restaurant—often a McDonald's—every day. However, whether McDonald's can actually be blamed as contributing to obesity rates remains a hotly debated topic, with strong arguments on both sides. The controversy highlights the contentious nature of the obesity debate, as analysts argue about the causes of obesity, the extent of the problem, and how best to address it.

A number of people have accused McDonald's of contributing to obesity by misrepresenting the healthfulness of its food. They believe that the company entices consumers into buying its food without warning them that eating it may cause them to gain weight. For example, in 2002, Caesar Barber brought a lawsuit against a number of fast food companies, including McDonald's, claiming that the companies engaged in deceptive advertising. "Those people in the advertisements don't really tell you what's in the food," said Barber. "It's all fat, fat and more fat. Now I'm obese." Attorney Samuel Hirsch agrees. In a 2002 lawsuit against McDonald's he argued that, "McDonald's Corp. engages in the distribution, sale and marketing of food products that are high in fat, salt, sugar and cholesterol content, which numerous studies have shown cause obesity . . . and other detrimental and adverse health effects. McDonald's failed to warn the users and consumers of their food products of the nature of these ingredients." In addition, charged Hirsch, not only did they fail to warn about the dangers of their food but, he claims, "McDonald's marketed its food as nutritious."

Critics of McDonald's are particularly incensed by what they see as the fast food chain's attempts to target children. They believe that the company takes advantage of impressionable children in its marketing campaigns, attempting to make McDonald's food a regular part of their diet. According to some commentators, humans develop their tastes at an early age and have difficulty changing them. By getting young children to enjoy its food, they argue, McDonald's is very likely to keep them as customers for the rest of their lives. Attorney Ralph Nader criticizes the way that McDonald's focuses its advertising on children for this purpose. "Much of McDonald's $3 billion a year television ad budget is directed toward children," he contends. "This fast food company does not force children to eat its junk food; it is far more effective to seduce them with toys and Ronald McDonald fun and tasty feelings, into clamoring for this bad and deadly diet that will plague them later in life." Numerous studies show that children who become obese are very likely to suffer from obesity and its related health problems for the rest of their lives.

However, while critics of McDonald's are numerous, so are supporters, who argue that while its food may be unhealthful, the company is simply providing what consumers demand. The analysts stress the importance of personal responsibility in preventing obesity, maintaining that there is no justification for criticizing McDonald's because ultimately a person can blame no one but him- or herself for becoming obese. Journalist Doug Bandow argues that "the most fundamental issue [in obesity] . . . is individual responsibility. . . . Big Macs do not leap into the mouths of unwilling consumers." Journalist Cal Thomas agrees. "If I stuff my face with Big Macs," writes Thomas, "why should the fast food chains be held liable? They didn't force feed me." As journalist Clarence Page points out, not only are fast food restaurants not force-feeding their customers, but they have actually provided nutritional information about their products and healthy menu options—options that customers have deliberately ignored. "Major fast food chains already make numerous nutrition information available on demand to anybody who wants it," claims Page. "The bigger question is, who wants it? McDonald's offers salads, for example, but they don't fly out of their coolers nearly as briskly as the cheeseburgers fly off the grill." One example of McDonald's failed attempt to provide healthier food is the McLean Deluxe, introduced in the early 1990s, which was marketed as healthy. The product was essentially ignored by consumers, who opted for less-healthful menu items.

Those who think that attacks on fast food companies are misguided also argue that while children cannot be expected to possess the same knowledge about health or have the same self-control that adults do, it is parents, not McDonald's, that deserve the blame for childhood obesity. Philip Fischer, a pediatrician at the Mayo Clinic in Rochester, Minnesota, believes that childhood obesity is often a result of children mimicking the unhealthy habits of their parents. "Parents play a vital role in the development of their children," he says. "Don't order french fries if you don't want your kids ordering french fries. Don't buy Oreos if you don't want your kids sneaking a few of them from the cookie jar. Likewise, your child will be more willing to snack on fruits and vegetables after seeing you doing the same." An anonymous respondent at Parent Soup, a Web site that offers advice for parents, echoes Fischer's advice. In her opinion, McDonald's has become a scapegoat for parents who have made bad diet and exercise choices for themselves and their children. "It is ridiculous [to blame McDonald's for obesity]," she asserts. "Everyone has to take responsibility for their own actions. . . . Parents are just looking for a scapegoat because of something that happened because it was their fault that their children are in that situation."

As the controversy over McDonald's illustrates, obesity is a highly contentious issue. The authors in *Opposing Viewpoints: Obesity* explore the topic of obesity in the following chapters: Is Obesity a Serious Problem? What Causes Obesity? What Is the Most Effective Way to Reduce Obesity? and Who Should Take Responsibility for Obesity? While there remain a multitude of opinions regarding these questions, the answers are vitally important as society begins to feel the impact of increasing obesity rates.

CHAPTER 1

Is Obesity a Serious Problem?

Chapter Preface

According to the American Diabetes Association (ADA), 6.3 percent of the American population suffers from diabetes. This disease is a major cause of blindness, kidney failure, and leg amputations. It greatly increases the risk of heart disease and stroke, and is estimated to be one of the top ten causes of death in developed nations.

The majority of diabetes cases—90 to 95 percent, estimates the ADA—are type 2 diabetes, in which the body does not properly use insulin, a hormone that is needed to convert sugar, starches, and other food into energy needed for daily life. Type 2 diabetes is most commonly caused by obesity and lack of physical activity, many experts contend. The link between obesity and diseases such as diabetes is one of the central subjects discussed when experts argue about whether obesity is a serious problem. While many health experts argue that obesity causes many diseases, others contend that this cause-and-effect relationship has never been proven.

Statistics show that as obesity has increased steadily in recent years, rates of type 2 diabetes have also risen sharply. This trend is most clearly seen in the United States. According to the National Institutes of Health, from 1960 to 2000, the percentage of obese American adults under the age of seventy-five more than doubled, and childhood obesity reached approximately 15 percent. In March 2004 the *Journal of the American Medical Association* reported that diabetes has also risen about 50 percent since the 1980s. Formerly called "adult-onset diabetes," because it was rarely seen in anyone under forty, type 2 diabetes now commonly occurs in children as young as eight, according to ADA president Francine R. Kaufman.

As obesity rates in the United States and other countries rise, debate about obesity's effects on health intensify. The majority of researchers warn that increasing obesity is leading to a health crisis. However, skeptics claim that connections between obesity rates and illness have been grossly exaggerated. Authors in the following chapter present various arguments on the connection between obesity and health problems such as diabetes.

"Obesity . . . is a major contributor to the global burden of chronic disease and disability."

Increasing Obesity Rates Are Causing a Growing Number of Health Problems Worldwide

World Health Organization

In the following viewpoint the World Health Organization claims that obesity has reached epidemic proportions worldwide, affecting large percentages of the global population in both developed and developing nations. Because obesity causes numerous serious health problems, argues the organization, this increase means it has become a major cause of health problems around the globe. Health problems caused by obesity include heart disease, diabetes, and some types of cancer, according to the organization. The World Health Organization is the United Nations' specialized agency for health. It works to help all peoples attain the highest possible level of health.

As you read, consider the following questions:

1. According to the organization, how do rising incomes and urbanization contribute to obesity?
2. What do studies show about people who are undernourished in early life then become obese in adulthood, as explained by the author?
3. What percentage of total health costs does obesity account for, according to the organization?

World Health Organization, "Obesity and Overweight," www.who.org, 2004.
Copyright © 2004 by the World Health Organization. All rights reserved.
Reproduced by permission.

Facts

- Globally, there are more than 1 billion overweight adults, at least 300 million of them obese.
- Obesity and overweight pose a major risk for chronic diseases, including type 2 diabetes, cardiovascular disease, hypertension and stroke, and certain forms of cancer.
- The key causes are increased consumption of energy-dense foods high in saturated fats and sugars, and reduced physical activity.

Obesity has reached epidemic proportions globally, with more than 1 billion adults overweight—at least 300 million of them clinically obese—and is a major contributor to the global burden of chronic disease and disability. Often coexisting in developing countries with under-nutrition, obesity is a complex condition, with serious social and psychological dimensions, affecting virtually all ages and socioeconomic groups.

Increased consumption of more energy-dense, nutrient-poor foods with high levels of sugar and saturated fats, combined with reduced physical activity, have led to obesity rates that have risen three-fold or more since 1980 in some areas of North America, the United Kingdom, Eastern Europe, the Middle East, the Pacific Islands, Australasia and China. The obesity epidemic is not restricted to industrialized societies; this increase is often faster in developing countries than in the developed world.

Obesity and overweight pose a major risk for serious diet-related chronic diseases, including type 2 diabetes, cardiovascular disease, hypertension and stroke, and certain forms of cancer. The health consequences range from increased risk of premature death, to serious chronic conditions that reduce the overall quality of life. Of especial concern is the increasing incidence of child obesity.

Why Is This Happening?

The rising epidemic reflects the profound changes in society and in behavioural patterns of communities over recent decades. While genes are important in determining a person's susceptibility to weight gain, energy balance is determined by calorie intake and physical activity. Thus societal changes and worldwide nutrition transition are driving the obesity epidemic. Economic growth, modernization, urbanization and globalization of food markets are just some of the forces thought to underlie the epidemic.

As incomes rise and populations become more urban, diets high in complex carbohydrates give way to more varied diets with a higher proportion of fats, saturated fats and sugars. At the same time, large shifts towards less physically demanding work have been observed worldwide. Moves towards less physical activity are also found in the increasing use of automated transport, technology in the home, and more passive leisure pursuits.

How Do We Define Obesity and Overweight?

The prevalence of overweight and obesity is commonly assessed by using body mass index (BMI), defined as the weight in kilograms divided by the square of the height in metres (kg/m2). A BMI over 25 kg/m2 is defined as overweight, and a BMI of over 30 kg/m2 as obese. These markers provide common benchmarks for assessment, but the risks of disease in all populations can increase progressively from lower BMI levels.

Adult mean BMI levels of 22–23 kg/m2 are found in Africa and Asia, while levels of 25–27 kg/m2 are prevalent across North America, Europe, and in some Latin American, North African and Pacific Island countries. BMI increases amongst middle-aged and elderly people, who are at the greatest risk of health complications. In countries undergoing nutrition transition,[1] overnutrition often co-exists with undernutrition. People with a BMI below 18.5 kg/m2 tend to be underweight.

The distribution of BMI is shifting upwards in many populations. And recent studies have shown that people who were undernourished in early life and then become obese in adulthood, tend to develop conditions such as high blood pressure, heart disease and diabetes at an earlier age and in more severe form than those who were never undernourished.

Currently [2004] more than 1 billion adults are overweight

---

1. changes in diet resulting from industrialization, urbanization, and economic development

—and at least 300 million of them are clinically obese. Current obesity levels range from below 5% in China, Japan and certain African nations, to over 75% in urban Samoa. But even in relatively low prevalence countries like China, rates are almost 20% in some cities.

Childhood obesity is already epidemic in some areas and on the rise in others. An estimated 22 million children under five are estimated to be overweight worldwide. According to the US Surgeon General, in the USA the number of overweight children has doubled and the number of overweight adolescents has trebled since 1980. The prevalence of obese children aged 6-to-11 years has more than doubled since the 1960s. Obesity prevalence in youths aged 12–17 has increased dramatically from 5% to 13% in boys and from 5% to 9% in girls between 1966–70 and 1988–91 in the USA. The problem is global and increasingly extends into the developing world; for example, in Thailand the prevalence of obesity in 5-to-12 year old children rose from 12.2% to 15.6% in just two years.

Obesity accounts for 2–6% of total health care costs in several developed countries; some estimates put the figure as high as 7%. The true costs are undoubtedly much greater as not all obesity-related conditions are included in the calculations.

How Does Excess Body Fat Impact Health?

Overweight and obesity lead to adverse metabolic effects on blood pressure, cholesterol, triglycerides and insulin resistance. Some confusion of the consequences of obesity arise because researchers have used different BMI cut-offs, and because the presence of many medical conditions involved in the development of obesity may confuse the effects of obesity itself.

The non-fatal, but debilitating health problems associated with obesity include respiratory difficulties, chronic musculoskeletal problems, skin problems and infertility. The more life-threatening problems fall into four main areas: CVD [cardiovascular disease] problems; conditions associated with insulin resistance such as type 2 diabetes; certain types of cancers, especially the hormonally related and large-bowel cancers; and gallbladder disease.

The likelihood of developing type 2 diabetes and hypertension rises steeply with increasing body fatness. Confined to older adults for most of the 20th century, this disease now affects obese children even before puberty. Approximately 85% of people with diabetes are type 2, and of these, 90% are obese or overweight. And this is increasingly becoming a developing world problem. In 1995, the Emerging Market Economies[2] had the highest number of diabetics. If current trends continue, India and the Middle Eastern crescent will have taken over by 2025. Large increases would also be observed in China, Latin America and the Caribbean, and the rest of Asia.

Exporting Obesity

Despite the magazine covers and frontpage stories, America can no longer claim obesity as its own personal disease.

The World Health Organization has reported that more than half of the populations in Spain, Australia, Brazil, Mexico, Denmark, Italy and Russia are overweight. In Germany alone, the annual cost of obesity has been estimated at $10 billion. Obesity is showing up in Papua New Guinea and Guatemala and China and South Korea and South Africa and Egypt.

Most observers blame two American exports—cheap fast food and high technology. They say we have enticed the world's peoples into eating Big Macs and Fritos while parking their rears in front of computers and televisions.

Joan Ryan, *Liberal Opinion Week*, April 5, 2004.

Raised BMI also increases the risks of cancer of the breast, colon, prostate, endometrium, kidney and gallbladder. Chronic overweight and obesity contribute significantly to osteoarthritis, a major cause of disability in adults. Although obesity should be considered a disease in its own right, it is also one of the key risk factors for other chronic diseases together with smoking, high blood pressure and high blood cholesterol. In the analyses carried out for World Health Report 2002, approximately 58% of diabetes and 21% of ischaemic heart disease[3] and 8–42% of certain cancers globally were attributable to a BMI above 21 kg/m2.

---

2. countries whose economies are becoming stronger and more competitive in global markets   3. This disease is caused by reduced blood supply to the heart.

What Can We Do About It?

Effective weight management for individuals and groups at risk of developing obesity involves a range of long-term strategies. These include prevention, weight maintenance, management of co-morbidities[4] and weight loss. They should be part of an integrated, multi-sectoral, population-based approach, which includes environmental support for healthy diets and regular physical activity. Key elements include:

- Creating supportive population-based environments through public policies that promote the availability and accessibility of a variety of low-fat, high-fibre foods, and that provide opportunities for physical activity.
- Promoting healthy behaviours to encourage, motivate and enable individuals to lose weight by:
  —eating more fruit and vegetables, as well as nuts and whole grains;
  —engaging in daily moderate physical activity for at least 30 minutes;
  —cutting the amount of fatty, sugary foods in the diet;
  —moving from saturated animal-based fats to unsaturated vegetable-oil based fats.
- Mounting a clinical response to the existing burden of obesity and associated conditions through clinical programmes and staff training to ensure effective support for those affected to lose weight or avoid further weight gain.

4. diseases caused by obesity

"The current war on fat is an irrational outburst of cultural hysteria, unsupported by sound science."

Increasing Obesity Rates Are Not Causing a Growing Number of Health Problems Worldwide

Paul Campos

In the following viewpoint Paul Campos challenges claims that obesity is a serious worldwide health problem. He maintains that such claims are not supported by scientific evidence. According to Campos, health officials and scientists distort research findings by ignoring confounding variables and adopting flexible standards of proof in order to advance the false belief that an obesity epidemic threatens health around the world. Campos is a professor of law at the University of Colorado and author of *The Obesity Myth*.

As you read, consider the following questions:

1. As cited by the author, what do the records of nearly 2 million Norwegians reveal about body weight and health?
2. According to Campos, why can nobody say whether fat people who slim down and stay slim are healthier in the long run?
3. What cultural and political factors have distorted scientific enquiry about obesity, as argued by the author?

Paul Campos, "Why Our Fears About Fat Are Misplaced: The War on Obesity Is Based Not on Sound Science but on Medical Self-Interest and Cultural Hysteria," *New Scientist*, vol. 182, May 1, 2004. Copyright © 2004 by Reed Elsevier Business Publishing, Ltd. Reproduced by permission.

Fat, flab, adipose tissue: call it what you will, it is one of the great obsessions of our age. In the early 1980s, stories about obesity were running in the world's major English-language media at the modest rate of about one per week. By 2003, reports sociologist Abigail Saguy from the University of California at Los Angeles, the figure had expanded to nearly 20 per day. We are in the throes of an unprecedented "obesity epidemic", doctors, scientists and health organisations repeatedly tell us.

Well, people certainly have been getting fatter in many countries. But here's the conundrum: overall health and life expectancy in these nations continues to improve. Take the US. Between 1990 and 2002 life expectancy here rose from 75.2 to 77.4 years, even though the nation's obesity rate rose, according to the Centers for Disease Control and Prevention, by 61 per cent. Indeed over that same period, the incidence of type 2 diabetes, the supposed bete noire of rising obesity levels, hardly changed, while death rates from heart disease, hypertension and some cancers actually dropped.

Perhaps the timebomb has yet to go off: public health officials often claim we are "about" to see the devastating consequences of obesity. Yet their predecessors were making the same claims 50 years ago—and indeed according to current definitions nearly half the American population was overweight as long ago as 1960.

No Evidence That Obesity Is a Health Risk

So what else is going on that might explain the conundrum? In the past few years I have been taking a close look at the claims of those who warn of the supposedly impending global calamity of the obesity epidemic. I have sought out the studies and findings behind the public health pronouncements, and canvassed views from a wide range of experts on what they really reveal. What I have found may prove hard for some to swallow: save for exceptions involving truly extreme cases, the medical literature simply does not support the claim that higher than average weight is a significant independent health risk.

What it actually demonstrates is, first, that the association between increased weight and increased health risk is weak, and disappears altogether when confounding variables are taken into account; and second, that public health programmes which attempt to make "overweight" and "obese" people thinner are, for a variety of reasons, likely to do more harm than good. In short, the current war on fat is an irrational outburst of cultural hysteria, unsupported by sound science.

Sceptical? Here are some statistics from what was, in the 1980s, the world's largest ever epidemiological study. From records of nearly 2 million Norwegians spanning a decade, it found the highest life expectancy among people with a body mass index (BMI) of 26 to 28—people who were solidly overweight, according to definitions now used by, among others, the World Health Organization [WHO] and the American public health establishment. Furthermore, the study found people with a BMI of 18 to 20 (almost all of whom these same institutions would classify as "ideally thin") had a lower life expectancy than those with BMIs between 34 and 36: who under current classifications were 60 to 75 pounds (25 to 35 kilograms) overweight, and therefore seriously obese.

As my book *The Obesity Myth* describes in detail, these statistics are typical of such studies. Large-scale studies consistently find little or no increase in mortality risk associated with weight, except at statistical extremes. Indeed, many such studies find the lowest mortality rates among supposedly overweight people, and a higher mortality risk among people who are five pounds "underweight" than among those who are supposedly 75 pounds overweight. And even these modest associations disappear when variables other than weight are taken into account. BMI figures correlate with increased mortality risk only among sedentary individuals: people who maintain quite modest activity levels show no such correlation.

But aren't fat people who slim down and stay slim healthier in the long run? Nobody can say, because no long-term study has tested the notion. And why not? For the simple reason that researchers have been unable to produce significant long-term weight loss in statistically meaningful numbers of people. Researchers repeatedly find instead that for the vast majority of people the long-term result of attempts to lose weight is "weight cycling"—repeatedly losing weight and then putting it on again. And that, as numerous studies have found, is no recipe for long-term health. For example, the famous Framingham study in the US found a strong correlation between weight cycling and mortality, and no increased risk among obese people who did not weight cycle.

Troubling "Evidence"

When it comes to the war on obesity, faulty interpretations of scientific data are rampant. . . .

Even respected doctors tout reams of numbers showing correlations between fat and heart disease or cancer to support the obesity crisis. But just because a group of fat people have certain health problems does not mean that their *weight* caused the problems. It's like concluding that since everyone who has cancer once ate a pink cupcake, that pink cupcakes cause cancer. It could have been a zillion other things.

Likewise, many studies merely crunch numbers to arrive at associations, or combine obesity with mortality figures for diabetes or heart disease because of their "belief" that fatness caused these conditions. Those involving clinical trials to demonstrate obesity-related causation are far and few between. Only two conditions have been proven to be directly caused by obesity, points out Paul Ernsberger, Ph.D., of Case Western Reserve School of Medicine [Ohio]: osteoarthritis of weight-bearing joints and uterine cancer due to obese women's higher estrogen levels and absence of proper medical attention.

Sandy Szwarc, www.techcentralstation.com, July 30, 2003.

Given all this, how do the public health officials who wage the increasingly intense war on fat support their arguments? The answer should disturb anyone who believes science is immune to the effects of economic and ideological bias. For on close inspection, the current panic over obesity is based on a severe distortion of scientific data.

Overstating Findings

The distortion tends to take one of three common forms. The first goes to the heart of the nature of epidemiology, which is, in the words of Harvard researcher Charles Hennekens, "a crude and inexact science". Epidemiologists, he says, "tend to overstate findings, either because we want attention or more grant money". (Ironically it is Hennekens whose work has been exploited by some of the worst fomenters of fat panic.)

Large-scale observational studies can never control for more than a few of the many factors that might explain the associations they observe between risk factors and disease, so epidemiologists who are careful not to overstate their findings will point to the dangers of attributing causal significance to small risk associations. A common rule of thumb is to view with suspicion any factor that fails to at least double relative risk, especially when the baseline risk is small.

Yet in the case of obesity, such caution is routinely abandoned. Health officials and researchers all too often treat small risks as presumptively causal. One recent study, for example, found a 13 per cent increased risk of post-menopausal breast cancer associated with being overweight. It added up to just one extra death per 10,000 "overweight" women per year. The authors still treated the finding as strong evidence of a causal relationship between weight and cancer.

Ignoring Confounding Variables

A second way in which health officials—and some researchers —routinely distort the facts on obesity is through ignoring confounding variables. There is overwhelming evidence that many causes of ill-health disproportionately affect the heavier than average—sedentary lifestyle, nutrition, weight cycling, poverty, access to and discrimination in healthcare, social discrimination generally. Yet many prominent obesity researchers prefer instead to pin the blame exclusively on body fat.

A particularly egregious example of this is a famous study that appeared in the *Journal of the American Medical Association (JAMA)* in 1999, which concluded that excess weight was killing 300,000 Americans per year. This "fact" has been cited more than 1700 times in the major English-language media over the last two years alone. In their statement of methods, the authors noted: "Our calculations assume that all (controlling for age, sex and smoking) excess mortality in obese people is due to their adiposity." While assuming the validity of one's conclusion certainly simplifies the process of scientific investigation, research ought to be about more than confirming hypotheses through circular reasoning.

The final distortion is to adopt flexible standards of proof. When those prosecuting the war on fat encounter findings that appear to confirm their views, they often dismiss any attempt to question them as ignorant, irrational or biased. Yet with findings that contradict their views, this confident positivism vanishes. The contradictory findings are explained away by an almost endless assortment of methodological caveats.

This leaping back and forth between uncritical faith and profound scepticism is particularly striking when researchers perform interpretive acrobatics with their own findings. For example, the authors of a 2003 *JAMA* study concluded that it provided compelling evidence of the deadly effects of higher than average weight. The study actually found negligible mortality increases among whites with BMIs up to the mid-30s, and no evidence of elevated mortality rates among black Americans across the "overweight" range (BMI 25 to 30). Indeed, among black women, no extra mortality risk was observed until a BMI of 37. But an accompanying editorial, by JoAnn Manson of the Harvard Medical School, commented that "it would be a great disservice to blacks if these results were used to promulgate the concept that excess weight is not harmful to them".

Distorting Scientific Enquiry

Ultimately, the current panic over increasing body mass has little to do with science, and everything to do with cultural and political factors that distort scientific enquiry. Among those factors are greed (consensus panels put together by organisations such as the WHO that have declared obesity a major health crisis are often made up wholly of doctors who run diet clinics), and cultural anxieties about social overconsumption in general.

Consider this. While the average American is about eight pounds heavier than in 1990, the average American car now weighs several hundred pounds more than it did in that year. Which statistic has more relevance to the world's long-term health?

"Overweight and obesity may not be infectious diseases, but they have reached epidemic proportions in the United States."

The United States Is Experiencing an Obesity Epidemic

U.S. Department of Health and Human Services

Obesity is a widespread and serious problem in the United States, according to the U.S. Department of Health and Human Services in the following viewpoint, which was excerpted from a 2001 report by the surgeon general. As measured by the body mass index, rates of obesity have increased for all ages, races, and genders in America, the department states, with the highest increases seen in minority and lower-income groups. The authors believe that action must be taken to reduce obesity and prevent an approaching health crisis. The U.S. Department of Health and Human Services is the U.S. government's principal agency for protecting the health of all Americans.

As you read, consider the following questions:

1. According to the department, approximately how many deaths each year in the United States are associated with being overweight or obese?
2. As explained by the authors, what are the possible limitations of the body mass index?
3. How is the prevalence of obesity and overweight related to age, according to the report?

U.S. Department of Health and Human Services, "The Surgeon General's Call to Action to Prevent and Decrease Overweight and Obesity," www.surgeongeneral. gov, 2001.

The 20th century saw remarkable and unprecedented improvements in the lives of the people of our country. We saw the infant mortality rate plummet and life expectancy increase by 30 years. Deaths from infectious diseases dropped tremendously, and improvements in medical care allowed many individuals with chronic disease to lead longer, fuller lives. Yet despite these and other successes, complex new health challenges continue to confront us.

Overweight and obesity are among the most important of these new health challenges. Our modern environment has allowed these conditions to increase at alarming rates and become highly pressing health problems for our Nation. At the same time, by confronting these conditions, we have tremendous opportunities to prevent the unnecessary disease and disability that they portend for our future. . . .

Overweight and obesity may not be infectious diseases, but they have reached epidemic proportions in the United States. Overweight and obesity are increasing in both genders and among all population groups. In 1999, an estimated 61 percent of U.S. adults were overweight or obese, and 13 percent of children and adolescents were overweight. Today [2001] there are nearly twice as many overweight children and almost three times as many overweight adolescents as there were in 1980. We already are seeing tragic results from these trends. Approximately 300,000 deaths a year in this country are currently associated with overweight and obesity. Left unabated, overweight and obesity may soon cause as much preventable disease and death as cigarette smoking.

Overweight and obesity have been grouped as one of the Leading Health Indicators in *Healthy People 2010*, the Nation's health objectives for the first decade of the 21st century. The Leading Health Indicators reflect the major public health concerns and opportunities in the United States. While we have made dramatic progress over the last few decades in achieving so many of our health goals, the statistics on overweight and obesity have steadily headed in the wrong direction. If this situation is not reversed, it could wipe out the gains we have made in areas such as heart disease, diabetes, several forms of cancer, and other chronic health problems.

Unfortunately, excessive weight for height is a risk factor for all of these conditions. . . .

BMI

The first challenge in addressing overweight and obesity lies in adopting a common public health measure of these conditions. An expert panel, convened by the National Institutes of Health (NIH) in 1998, has utilized Body Mass Index (BMI) for defining overweight and obesity. BMI is a practical measure that requires only two things: accurate measures of an individual's weight and height. BMI is a measure of weight in relation to height. BMI is calculated as weight in pounds divided by the square of the height in inches, multiplied by 703. Alternatively, BMI can be calculated as weight in kilograms divided by the square of the height in meters.

Studies have shown that BMI is significantly correlated with total body fat content for the majority of individuals. BMI has some limitations, in that it can overestimate body fat in persons who are very muscular, and it can underestimate body fat in persons who have lost muscle mass, such as many elderly. Many organizations, including over 50 scientific and medical organizations that have endorsed the NIH *Clinical Guidelines*, support the use of a BMI of 30 kg/m^2 or greater to identify obesity in adults and a BMI between 25 kg/m^2 and 29.9 kg/m^2 to identify overweight in adults. These definitions are based on evidence that suggests health risks are greater at or above a BMI of 25 kg/m^2 compared to those at a BMI below that level. The risk of death, although modest until a BMI of 30 kg/m^2 is reached increases with an increasing Body Mass Index. . . .

The United States is experiencing substantial increases in overweight and obesity (as defined by a BMI $\geq$ 25 for adults) that cut across all ages, racial and ethnic groups, and both genders. According to self-reported measures of height and weight, obesity (BMI $\geq$ 30) has been increasing in every State in the Nation. Based on clinical height and weight measurements in the 1999 National Health and Nutrition Examination Survey (NHANES), 34 percent of U.S. adults aged 20 to 74 years are overweight (BMI 25 to 29.9), and an additional 27 percent are obese (BMI $\geq$ 30). This contrasts with the late

1970s, when an estimated 32 percent of adults aged 20 to 74 years were overweight, and 15 percent were obese.

The most recent data (1999) estimate that 13 percent of children aged 6 to 11 years and 14 percent of adolescents aged 12 to 19 years are overweight. During the past two decades, the percentage of children who are overweight has nearly doubled (from 7 to 13 percent), and the percentage of adolescents who are overweight has almost tripled (from 5 to 14 percent).

Disparities in Prevalence

Between the second and third National Health and Nutrition Examination Surveys (NHANES II and III), the prevalence of overweight and obesity (BMI ≥ 25 for adults and ≥ 95th percentile for age and gender in children) increased in both genders, across all races and ethnicities, and across all age groups. Disparities in overweight and obesity prevalence exist in many segments of the population based on race and ethnicity, gender, age, and socioeconomic status. For example, overweight and obesity are particularly common among minority groups and those with a lower family income.

Race and Ethnicity, Gender, and Age

In general, the prevalence of overweight and obesity is higher in women who are members of racial and ethnic minority populations than in non-Hispanic white women. Among men, Mexican Americans have a higher prevalence of overweight and obesity than non-Hispanic whites or non-Hispanic blacks. For non-Hispanic men, the prevalence of overweight and obesity among whites is slightly greater than among blacks.

Within racial groups, gender disparities exist, although not always in the same direction. Based on NHANES III (1988–1994), the proportion of non-Hispanic black women who were overweight or obese (BMI ≥ 25; 69 percent) was higher than the proportion of non-Hispanic black men (58 percent). For non-Hispanic whites, on the other hand, the proportion of men who were overweight or obese (BMI ≥ 25; 62 percent) exceeded the proportion of women (47 percent). However, when looking at obesity alone (BMI ≥ 30), the prevalence was slightly higher in non-Hispanic white women compared to non-Hispanic white men (23 percent and 21 percent, respectively). The prevalence of overweight or obesity (BMI ≥ 25) was about the same in Mexican American men and women (69 percent and 70 percent, respectively). Although smaller surveys indicate a higher prevalence of overweight and obesity in American Indians, Alaska Natives, and Pacific Islander Americans and a lower prevalence in Asian Americans compared to the general population, the number surveyed in NHANES III was too small to reliably report prevalence comparisons of overweight and obesity for these populations.

THE EVOLUTION OF HOMO OVEREATUS AMERICANUS

SOUTH FLORIDA SUN-SENTINEL

Lowe. © by Tribune Media Services. Reproduced by permission.

Racial and ethnic disparities in overweight may also occur in children and adolescents. Data for youth from NHANES III showed a similar pattern to that seen among adults. Mexican American boys tended to have a higher prevalence of overweight than non-Hispanic black and non-Hispanic white boys. Non-Hispanic black girls tended to have a higher prevalence of overweight compared to non-Hispanic white and Mexican American girls. The National Heart, Lung, and Blood Institute Growth and Health Study on overweight in children found a higher mean BMI for black girls aged 9 and

10 years, compared to white girls of the same ages. This racial difference in BMI widened and was even greater at age 19.

In addition to racial and ethnic and gender disparities, the prevalence of overweight and obesity also varies by age. Among both men and women, the prevalence of overweight and obesity increases with advancing age until the sixth decade, after which it starts to decline.

Socioeconomic Status

Disparities in the prevalence of overweight and obesity also exist based on socioeconomic status. For all racial and ethnic groups combined, women of lower socioeconomic status (income ≤ 130 percent of poverty threshold) are approximately 50 percent more likely to be obese than those with higher socioeconomic status (income > 130 percent of poverty threshold). Men are about equally likely to be obese whether they are in a low or high socioeconomic group.

Among children, the relationship between socioeconomic status and overweight in girls is weaker than it is in women; that is, girls from lower income families have not consistently been found to be overweight compared to girls from higher income families. Among Mexican American and non-Hispanic black children and adolescents, family income does not reliably predict overweight prevalence. However, non-Hispanic white adolescents from lower income families experience a greater prevalence of overweight than those from higher income families. . . .

Current knowledge is clear on many issues: the prevalence of overweight and obesity is high, and that of obesity is increasing rapidly; adolescents who are overweight are at high risk of becoming overweight or obese adults; overweight and obesity increase the risk for serious diseases such as type 2 diabetes, hypertension, and high blood cholesterol; and overweight and obesity are associated with premature death and disability. It is also known that a healthy diet and adequate physical activity aid in maintaining a healthy weight and, among overweight or obese persons, can promote weight loss. . . .

Public health efforts are carried by the force of ideas and by the power of commitment. *Healthy People 2010* identifies goals to improve the country's health status, including reducing the prevalence of overweight and obesity. This *Surgeon General's Call to Action to Prevent and Decrease Overweight and Obesity* addresses the *Healthy People 2010* objectives to reduce the prevalence of overweight and obesity and presents many ideas by which this can be done. Translating these ideas into meaningful action will require a great commitment. We must collectively build on existing successful programs in both the public and private sectors, identify current gaps in action, and develop and initiate actions to fill those gaps. Public-private working groups should be formed around key themes or around the major settings in which obesity prevention and treatment efforts need to take place. While the magnitude of the problem is great, the range of potential solutions is even greater. The design of successful interventions and actions for prevention and management of overweight and obesity will require the careful attention of many individuals and organizations working together through multiple spheres of influence.

> *"The claim that obesity costs the United States $117 billion a year and kills 300,000 Americans annually . . . [is] seriously flawed."*

The United States Is Not Experiencing an Obesity Epidemic

Dan Mindus

The extent of the obesity problem in the United States has been greatly exaggerated, maintains Dan Mindus in the following viewpoint. According to Mindus, claims about the prevalence of obesity and obesity-related deaths are based on flawed studies that have produced inflated statistics. In addition, he argues, the body mass index, used to measure obesity, further inflates these numbers by incorrectly classifying many healthy individuals as obese. Mindus is a senior analyst at the Center for Consumer Freedom, an organization that works to promote personal responsibility and protect consumer choices.

As you read, consider the following questions:

1. According to Mindus, why did 39 million Americans wake up overweight in 1998?
2. In the author's opinion, what is wrong with the claim that obesity costs Americans more than $100 million a year?
3. Why does the American Obesity Organization promote faulty obesity statistics, as argued by Mindus?

A World Health Organization [WHO] panel recently concluded that a 5-foot-6 man or woman of Asian descent weighing 137 pounds should be considered "overweight." That would place the trim Hiroyuki Sanada, one of Tom Cruise's co-stars in "The Last Samurai" [movie], just a few pounds shy of this category.

Body Mass Index

Welcome to the politics of fat, where bathroom scales can be tax-deductible, lawyers are lining up to sue anything rumored to contain calories and the media have fed us a steady diet of hysteria and hyperbole. In this twilight zone of fat panic, something called the Body Mass Index (BMI) uses only our height and weight to divide us into categories: obese, overweight and government approved.

A BMI of 30 or more makes you "obese"; at 5-foot-7 and 201 pounds, Tom Cruise's magic number is 31. If the WHO gets its way, Asians will join the "last samurai" in the obese category if their BMI hits 26 (5-foot-7 and 163 pounds, for example). A BMI of just 22—perfectly "healthy" for most of us, even by WHO's ever-tightening standards—will make an Asian "overweight."

The global love-handle police insist on this ridiculous BMI standard, which classifies 61 percent of Americans as overweight or obese. You have probably heard that number. Along with the claim that obesity costs the United States $117 billion a year and kills 300,000 Americans annually, it is one of the three most commonly cited figures associated with our so-called obesity epidemic. But it's more like an epidemic of bad statistics. All three of these numbers are seriously flawed.

An Unreliable Measure

The federal Centers for Disease Control and Prevention acknowledge that these results are counterintuitive: "Overweight may or may not be due to increases in body fat. It may also be due to an increase in lean muscle." This explains why the new governor of California[1] (6-foot-2, 257 pounds, BMI

---

1. Arnold Schwarzenegger, elected in 2003

of 33) is officially obese, too. For the rest of us, however, the story is a bit more complicated. One night in 1998, more than 39 million Americans went to sleep at a government-approved weight and woke up "overweight," thanks to an arbitrary shift in the BMI cutoff for "overweight" status.

Oversimplifying Obesity

The body mass index . . . [is] a range. The CDC [Centers for Disease Control] says that many factors, including muscle mass, bone structure and family history must be considered. Body mass index is "only one piece of a personal health profile," according to the Web site. It's a screening device, after which one may decide whether to see a physician.

In other words, it's crude. Yet its crudeness does not prevent it from being applied to the entire population. Nor does it prevent the CDC and other health professionals from declaring that 64 percent of us are overweight and nearly half of that number, or about 30 percent, are obese, and that obesity has increased dramatically—in fact, doubled—in the past 20 years.

Calculating that increase is difficult because the data over time are not really comparable. The definition of obesity keeps changing. You may remember the day in the summer of 1998 when about 25 million Americans became overweight overnight. That was because the official definition of overweight changed—significantly. On one day, a man 5 feet, 10 inches tall weighing 184 pounds was normal. The next morning, he was nine pounds overweight.

The estimates of economic costs are even more crude. The medical literature says that most diseases connected with obesity tend to have multiple causes, some of which are indeterminate. Do you have sufficient faith in statisticians to believe that they can slice and dice the costs of these diseases and declare with any precision that obesity is responsible for X percent or Y percent versus, say, family history or smoking or air pollution or stress or hypertension?

Fred Barbash, *Washington Post*, September 15–21, 2003.

The standard that we abandoned in 1998 had the virtue of distinguishing between men and women—something we don't even attempt to do anymore. Now the WHO wants to start determining "acceptable" BMI levels according to race—making Jackie Chan (5-foot-8, 160 pounds, BMI 24) our latest "overweight" movie star.

Bogus Claims

The claim that excess weight kills 300,000 Americans each year is bizarre in its assumption that overweight people are officially immune to all other causes of death. As insane as it sounds, if Cruise were to kick the bucket for any reason, he would count toward the mythical 300,000 total.

The *New England Journal of Medicine* knows this is bogus. In an editorial, the journal's editors wrote that the 300,000 figure "is by no means well-established," and that it is "derived from weak or incomplete data." Still, this flawed number finds its way into nearly every public discussion about obesity—as does the spurious claim that obesity costs Americans more than $100 billion every year. That figure is derived from a single 1998 study published by the journal *Obesity Research*. This study had serious limitations. The authors acknowledged that their methods allowed for the "double-counting of costs" that "would inflate the cost estimate." They also admitted that "height and weight are not included in many of the primary data sources" that they relied upon.

Worse yet, these bean-counters used the wrong definition of obesity. Traditionally, a BMI of 30 or more makes you obese, but the authors decided to arbitrarily set their threshold at 29. A small error? Not at all. They wound up wrongly including the health costs of more than 10 million Americans.

Claims Built on Shaky Ground

Unfortunately, activist groups are all too happy to build their nutritional utopias on the shaky ground of these faulty obesity statistics. The guiltiest in the bunch are the self-described "food police" at the Center for Science in the Public Interest—the traditional advocates of "sin" taxes on foods they don't want you to eat. A health-advocacy group called the Physicians Committee for Responsible Medicine also uses these bogus stats to force a vegetarian diet down our collective throats. Then there's the American Obesity Association, which aggressively promotes these numbers in its quest to have obesity classified as a "disease"—for the financial gain of the manufacturers of the weight-loss drug and products who pay its bills.

Basic logic dictates that obesity is no more a disease than couch potato-itis, that replacing milk and chicken with tofu won't magically melt the pounds and that Tom Cruise isn't fat. But obesity scares and cooked numbers have tipped the scales against common sense.

*"There is something uniquely worrisome
. . . in . . . the cavalcade of new evidence
about obese and overweight children."*

Obesity in Children Is a Serious Problem

Mary Eberstadt

Child obesity is increasing dramatically around the world, maintains Mary Eberstadt in the following viewpoint. She argues that while adult obesity can be seen simply as a result of free choice, children's obesity cannot. In her opinion, rising childhood obesity is due to a lack of parental care, particularly from mothers who often work outside the home and no longer monitor their children's eating habits as closely as they once did. Obese children suffer from a large number of physical and mental health problems, Eberstadt contends. Eberstadt is a research fellow at the Hoover Institution, a public policy research center devoted to advanced study of politics, economics, and international affairs.

As you read, consider the following questions:
1. What do Canadian statistics show about the number of overweight children in Canada, as cited by Eberstadt?
2. What extra medical problems do overweight children suffer from, according to the author?
3. As explained by Eberstadt, why is heredity not a sufficient explanation for the increase in child obesity?

Mary Eberstadt, "The Child-Fat Problem," *Policy Review*, February/March 2003, pp. 3–10, 17–19. Copyright © 2003 by *Policy Review*. Reproduced by permission.

Just three months ago [in late 2002] a major study published in the *Journal of the American Medical Association* [*JAMA*] confirmed what any American with eyes even half-open could already have reported—that not only our adults, but also our children, are fat and getting fatter all the time. As the Department of Health and Human Services put it in a summary of this latest study's evidence, "Among children and teens ages 6 to 19, 15 percent (almost 9 million) are overweight according to the 1999–2000 data, or triple what the proportion was in 1980."

The widespread media attention given to this bad-news story would appear to be justified, for the *JAMA* study followed at least two other blue-chip examinations during the past year or so of the underage fat explosion. One of these, a report on the whopping economic costs of child and adolescent obesity, was published in *Pediatrics* magazine by researchers for the Centers for Disease Control (CDC). The other publication was a less prominent but also intriguing report in the May [2002] issue of the *Journal of Nutrition* written by researchers at the University of North Carolina [UNC]. This one emphasized one of the lesser-known aspects of the fat problem—that "adolescent obesity increases significantly among second- and third-generation immigrants to the United States," in the words of a UNC press release.

A Worldwide Problem

This is not to say that underage corpulence is unique to Americans and their offspring—far from it. Misconceptions and undeserved reputations to the contrary, most other advanced countries (and for that matter, a number of not-so-advanced ones) do indeed share in the child-fat-and-obesity problem, for the most part differing from us in degree rather than kind. In England, reported the *Guardian* earlier this year [2003], "Adult obesity rates have tripled and those in children have doubled since 1982." In Canada, says the *Globe and Mail*, also in 2002, "More than a third of Canadian children aged 2 to 11 are overweight, and half that number are obese, according to newly published Statistics Canada data." Moreover, "Canada now has more fat children than fat adults." As for Australia, a 2000 study there found that children of either sex were twice as likely to be defined as overweight in 2000 as in 1985.

Nor is the Anglo-speaking world the only one with a child-fat problem. Its svelte reputation quite aside, for example, continental Europe and its children are ballooning as well. In Italy, report researchers for the *Bollettino Epidemiologico Nazionale*, "Neapolitan children were more at risk of obesity than were children from France, Holland, the United States, and also than children living in Milan in northern Italy," while in the province of Benevento, "The prevalence of overweight and obesity was greater . . . than in England, Scotland, and the United States." In Germany, according to researchers in the *International Journal of Obesity*, a "large study on all children entering school in Bavaria in 1997 shows patterns of overweight and obesity which are comparable with other European data" (though still "lower than US and Australian data"). Even vaunted France, if the French National Institute of Health and Medical Research is to be believed, admits an obesity problem among 10-year-olds of "epidemic proportions." "The number of seriously overweight children in France," reports the same institute, "has more than doubled since the 1980's.". . .

A Uniquely Worrisome Problem

If free-choosing adults were the only people implicated thus, we could perhaps rest philosophical here, content in the knowledge that the fat problem—. . . like smoking—will ultimately right or at least ameliorate itself in the long run. The problem, however, as the latest round of headlines demonstrates, is that the casualty count goes beyond those with free choice. For there *is* something uniquely worrisome, both as a public health issue and as a social fact, in one important subset of that problem—namely, the cavalcade of new evidence about obese and overweight children.

Child fat, though obviously related to adult fat in a variety of debated ways, is nevertheless a different order of problem—as experts already agree and the public is only beginning to recognize. The many American adults who might arguably be said to weigh more than they "ought" are one thing. . . . As one of many risky behaviors in which adults manifestly take pleasure, overeating—like, say, drinking, smoking, drug-taking, and promiscuous sex—will have certain adverse consequences; these consequences will vary in seriousness according to how often and how long the risky behavior has been going on; and adults, though they may injure themselves by any and all of the above, are by common near-consensus qualified to make their own decisions about self-inflicted risks and injuries (subject to a certain measure of hectoring from others).

In fact, a compelling case can be made that of all the above-listed personal behaviors prone to abuse, adult fat is *least* injurious to the greater public good—even given the issue of its medical costs, which are surely more than offset by the fantastically successful diet and fitness industries which naturally exploit the problem. Excess weight, in and of itself, does not cause traffic accidents, wreck marriages, impair moral and social judgment, or cause upswings in communicable diseases. Moreover, one might bear in mind the fact that the "problem" of adult corpulence, while real, remains the sort of problem that much of the rest of humanity would like to have. "To be sure, obesity is a major health problem," as Stephen Moore put it recently on *National Review Online* (November 27, 2002). "But it is not nearly so problematic as the nutritional problem for most of mankind throughout the ages: chronic hunger and periodic famines." In sum, the fact that some half of American adults may be carrying around more pounds than their doctors think fit may not be what admirers mean by national greatness. But compared to a good many other social ills, adult fat would appear (except perhaps from the point of view of trial lawyers) more socially negligible.

Serious Problems for Obese Children

No such rationales, however, can be applied to the case of child and adolescent fat. As the *New York Times* put it the day after Thanksgiving in an editorial clearly reflecting the gravity of the phenomenon, "the issue has serious long-term implications. For the first time, children are being diagnosed with weight-related chronic ailments that usually strike much later in life, including hypertension and diabetes." Poignant evidence of the same appears particularly in the CDC report mentioned earlier, which documents the dramatic increase in obesity-linked hospitalizations for children—the doubling of diabetes diagnoses, the fivefold rise in sleep apnea cases, and the tripling of gall bladder disease admissions, all during the past two decades. The European and other national reports mentioned earlier note the same phenomenon; that is, the appearance in even very young obese children of diseases and disorders hitherto thought limited to older adults. And though a handful of contrarians have stepped forward in the *Atlantic Monthly*, the *New Republic*, and elsewhere to deny that American supersizing is either problematic or new, the facts about youngsters in particular quite obviously point otherwise. It is one thing to see shirtless obese children paraded like circus freaks on the Maury Povich show and to think the problem a subset of trash TV. It is another to read accounts written by actual doctors of what is suffered on account of this trend—the children who are so heavy that they routinely wake in panic because their windpipes have temporarily closed up; the growing incidence not only of early heart trouble but of fat-linked cancers in children only years removed from babyhood; the experiments, some of them parlous, with drugs and surgeries of all kinds to counter the unprecedented medical woes of overweight children. Whatever else may be said about them, the public health issues raised by child fat are no media inventions.

Moreover, even those children and teenagers who are merely heavy, rather than clinically obese, find their weight affecting them adversely in other ways—for example, by making exercise more arduous, and hence less likely. And there is also the troubling fact that fat children tend to grow up into fat adults. This means that the very personal health of those children who are fat today is a continued and lifelong battle.

There are other, extra-medical problems in store for such children as well. Less arresting from a public health perspective, but probably more so from the point of view of most actual children and teenagers, is the personal suffering endured by many overweight children. As if that suffering were not compelling enough in its own right, there are also long-standing and unanswered questions about possibly related problems: for example, the relationship later in life between the repeated drive to eat more than one ought and

Overweight Children and Teens

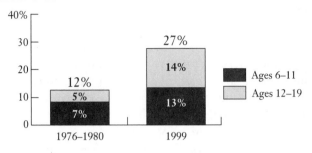

Percentage of U.S.
children or teens

CQ Researcher, January 31, 2003.

other forms of medically questionable oral compulsion, no-tably smoking and drinking.

Thus, though a range of opinion on the subject of fat does still exist within society at large—with poorer, black and Hispanic subgroups generally least likely to see child fat as a serious problem—the opinion of actual medical experts is by contrast virtually unanimous. For a constellation of physical and psychological reasons, most now believe that child obe-sity is no longer "simply a cosmetic problem," in the words of CDC lead researcher Dr. William Dietz, but "a serious medical problem" in itself. And while the poorest children, here as elsewhere in this vale of tears, are more likely to be burdened with the child-fat problem than are the rich, even the best-off children are participating too in the long caloric march, as the growth charts and weight charts and the de-clining age of menarche across class and race prove beyond doubt. In short, to switch metaphors, a rising tide of fat is rocking all our social and economic boats.

Heredity Does Not Explain the Facts

Naturally enough, and as most people also know, considerable industry has gone into pinpointing exactly how we came to live so large. From sociological observations about the simul-taneous explosion of American prosperity (we eat too much because we can) to more ideological anti-business analyses (we're fat because McDonald's rules our world), explanations of U.S. rotundity abound. Evolutionary biologists blame our survival-riveted "hardwiring"; dietitians, our meat-and-dairy intensive diet; advocates of breast-feeding, our reliance on the highly more caloric alternative of baby formula. Still other observers point naturally to the greatly diminished physicality of American life: the fact that vehicles rather than feet get most people where they want to go, that recess and other run-around time has been curtailed in schools around the country, that sedentary pursuits of television and electronic games are climbing alongside those juvenile body-mass indices.

At the moment, the explanation that appears to enjoy most support in the popular mind is that of heredity. . . .

Despite its surface appeal and current popularity, however, the argument from heredity is seriously limited, for reasons familiar to researchers. In essence, genetic programming alone cannot explain the great leap forward into heaviness and obesity these past two or three decades. If people were truly "blueprinted" to gain weight, then the obesity problem would presumably have developed many years earlier, as soon as they had access to extra food. In other words, most Americans (and other moderns) have been prosperous enough, for a long enough time, that they could have eaten themselves to today's weights long ago; for some reason, however, they did not. As the lead author of yet another 2002 study—this one in the *Annals of Internal Medicine*—told a reporter, "People born in 1964 who became obese did so about 25 to 27 percent faster than those born in 1957." Heredity cannot explain facts like these. . . .

Policing by Parents

Historically, either parents or extended family or both have controlled most of what and when children could eat. The fact that this control was typically born of necessity—i.e., of making sure there was enough to go around—does not confute its significance. After all, this parental or familial power has been exercised virtually everywhere in human history, from the savannah to the igloo to the Raj and back again. And it has been exercised by rich as well as poor, else the history of better-off social classes would be replete with the oversized children and adults we see today (as it markedly is not). Thus, the why underlying the child-fat problem can be formulated something like this: Given that parents and related adults across history and cultures have policed their children's eating habits, in what kind of social universe do adults cease to perform that task? The answer, which is as obvious as it is unwelcome, is that our universe has become one in which adults, particularly related adults in the form of parents, are not around to do the policing in the first place. In other words, there would appear to be an obvious relationship between absentee parents—meaning particularly, for reasons we will see, mothers—and overstuffed children. . . .

The idea that non-parental care plays a role in the child-fat problem is not only defensible, given the evidence, but is also intellectually satisfying on a couple of counts as other theories are not. For one thing, such a link would explain aspects of the child-fat problem that have so far eluded explanation. One is the fact that, as mentioned earlier and as is contrary to popular preconceptions, child fat and obesity are rising among most developed countries (where mothers are also typically out of the house), irrespective of differences in diet, culture, and the rest. Another is the fact that this link would also help explain why immigrant families in which mothers often work are at particularly high risk of becoming overweight.

The point here is not metaphysical, and it is not even intentionally contrarian. I mean only to draw attention to a pedestrian fact: that a parent or other responsible adult in the home can mean the difference between a supervised diet, on the one hand, and an auto-gluttonous free-for-all on the other. Common sense itself demands the recognition that these events are indeed related—that children are eating more because they are less likely to be around anyone, particularly an adult anyone, telling them that this is a bad idea. . . .

The Role of Mothers

It will be objected that more ought to be said about fathers in all this, and that mothers who are already busy to the point of exhaustion are being unfairly singled out for their offspring's good. Any mother, this author included, will heartily sympathize. Here as elsewhere, however, life is nakedly unfair. For reasons so deep as to be unplumbable, it is mothers, more than other adults in a child's life, who experience the felt need to police what their children eat and to cajole and order them into eating as the mother believes they "should." It is mothers, not others, who in general have the strongest opinions about these things—often vehement opinions, whether they are home with their children or not. Institutionalized care centers, whether day care or schools, use snacks and food for crowd-pleasing, if not crowd control. And even the best paid help is simply unlikely to be as attentive to what children eat as a mother would—for the long-term health of the child is not in fact the caregiver's chief concern (that, rather, is the short-term goal of keeping the child supervised and happy). Again, for reasons that remain as mysterious as they are intuitively obvious, it appears that mothers, more than any other figures in a child's life, are willing to risk the short-term gluttonous dissatisfaction of the child for the longer-term benefits of a better diet. Some readers no doubt will decry that formulation; the open-minded will acknowledge its domestic truth.

Filling a Void?

Deplored or not, the link to which current research is only beginning to draw attention stands as is: a Janus-faced sign-post showing the sunny side of our material wonderland, one in which everyone is free to leave home for the paid market-place, and the darker side of what that social exodus is leaving behind. . . . Maybe the "void" being "filled" by overeating, to use the intriguing terms of Overeaters Anonymous and other dietary theorists, is even more acute in young human beings than in others. Maybe a little more contact and companionship, with real rather than virtual parents and other family, might make them a little less ravenous.

> *"While 17 percent of whites fit the criteria
> for obesity, 27 percent of African
> Americans and 21 percent of Latinos are
> considered obese."*

Obesity Is a Serious Problem in Poor and Minority Communities

Silja J.A. Talvi

In the United States rates of obesity are highest in poor communities of color, argues Silja J.A. Talvi in the following viewpoint. According to Talvi, it is often difficult for individuals in these groups to make healthy diet choices because in the places they live they have more access to convenience stores than supermarkets, where fruits and vegetables are available. In addition, says Talvi, immigrant groups and Native Americans trying to adapt to mainstream American culture often become obese as they substitute the healthy foods of their cultures for fast food. Talvi is a freelance journalist who has written for a number of publications, including *In These Times* and the *Christian Science Monitor.*

As you read, consider the following questions:

1. According to the author, how does lack of private transportation contribute to obesity in poor neighborhoods?
2. What percent of actors on black prime time television are overweight, according to Talvi?
3. How does the "thrifty gene" theory explain obesity among Native Americans, as explained by the author?

Silja J.A. Talvi, "Bearing the Burden," *ColorLines*, vol. 5, Fall 2002, pp. 10–12. Copyright © 2002 by ColorLines Magazine. Reproduced by permission.

Althia Gauthier's mother was only 42 when she had a heart attack. A smoker with high blood pressure and a poor diet, Gauthier's mother had no idea what she was experiencing, no inkling that she was at risk for a heart attack at her age.

Instead of calling out for help, she lit up a cigarette and waited it out in a women's restroom. The heart attack didn't kill her, but lymphoma did, years later. Then Gauthier's father died from diabetes two years ago, largely from factors related to his diet and lifestyle.

Gauthier, one of 30 nurses nationally with advanced training in assessing heart disease risk in women, struggles with her own weight and high blood pressure.

"I don't want to have a heart attack at 42, like my mom did," says Gauthier, the care coordinator for the Tulane Xavier National Center of Excellence in Women's Health in New Orleans. "Some weeks I don't do all the things I need to do [to minimize my health risks], but I never stop trying."

From Gauthier's standpoint, it is imperative to keep trying to eat well and to get enough exercise, because the alternative is to join the ranks of a larger statistical trend of obesity—and related, chronic health conditions—now commonplace across the U.S., most acutely in communities of color.

While 17 percent of whites fit the criteria for obesity, 27 percent of African Americans and 21 percent of Latinos are considered obese, and therefore at increased risk for major health problems, including diabetes, asthma, hypertension and kidney and heart disease. (Altogether, nearly 300,000 deaths per year are now associated with obesity.)

People of color living at lower economic levels are even more likely to be obese: nearly 34 percent of African Americans and 25 percent of Latinos earning less than $10,000 are obese, compared with 19 percent of whites.

The problem of obesity in communities of color is not limited to Latinos and African Americans, however. Although Native Americans, Asian Americans and Pacific Islanders are not tracked as closely in obesity issues, it's known that roughly 60 percent of urban Indians are overweight, and that Samoans and Native Hawaiians frequently struggle with obesity and related health complications, particularly after moving to the mainland.

"The situation facing Indians here is very similar to what natives are dealing with in other areas," says Billy Rogers, director of the Native Wellness Institute in Norman, Oklahoma. "You make people feel bad about their culture, you take away their family systems, their lifestyle, and there are going to be very dramatic changes in people's diets and bodies.

"What I see are people who don't know who they are anymore, to a great extent," adds Rogers. "They've embraced the values of the dominant culture, which is a fast food culture. It's an 'I want it now and I don't have much patience' culture."

Over 60 percent of all Americans are now overweight, and experts agree that fast food, television, office jobs, lack of fresh fruits and vegetables in school lunches, and genetic factors have all conspired to make Americans of all ages fatter. But for people of color and poor people, the issues are even more complex and far-reaching.

Unhealthy Choices

According to a study published last year [2001] in the *American Journal of Preventive Medicine*, there are four times more supermarkets in predominantly white neighborhoods, compared to predominantly African American neighborhoods.

The University of North Carolina School of Medicine–funded study set out to study the prevalence of supermarkets, convenience stores, restaurants, and bars in a variety of neighborhoods in Mississippi, North Carolina, Maryland, and Minnesota. The study proved what many community activists and health care providers had known for years: poor, black neighborhoods have an excess of bars and convenience stores, and not enough places from which to buy healthier produce and foodstuffs.

The study also demonstrated that relatively few households in poor, African American neighborhoods had access to private transportation, making it even harder to obtain healthy food.

"There are fewer options for many of my patients in their neighborhoods," agrees Dr. Jeanette Newton Keith, assistant professor of clinical medicine and an attending physician at the University of Chicago Hospitals. "This is by far one of the most difficult challenges to overcome."

Dr. Keith, an African American physician and specialist in both gastroenterology and clinical nutrition, tries to encourage her patients to take public transportation to local farmers' markets, or to grow simple summer gardens for vegetables like tomatoes and cucumbers.

Food Roles

In talking about the real health risks facing women of color, Gauthier is careful to frame the topics of nutrition and exercise in ways that are both situationally and culturally relevant to the women who attend her Wellness Wednesdays sessions in New Orleans, which are tailored to address participants' pressing health questions and concerns.

"When we talk about women of color, we have to realize we're often talking about women with children, women with low incomes, and women who are in situations where the first thing on their mind is survival. It's not about 'how healthy I am,' but about 'how my child is going to be fed today.'"

Nutritional and calorie-cutting advice should be no different in this regard, notes Gauthier.

"We have communities, like the African American and Hispanic communities, where we celebrate with food," she explains. "When you tell us that we need to stop eating all these [foods] that we've grown up with, that are cultural in nature, that have made us feel good in the past . . . and then you tell us that these foods are killing us, you've got to think about the message we're receiving."

The message is far better received, Gauthier says, if it makes room for the role of food in celebrations, family reunions, and Sunday dinners, but advises people to avoid eating fat-laden dishes on a daily basis.

What's more, says José Camaro, health educator at La Clinica de la Raza in Oakland, California, telling people not to eat certain foods from their culture is an approach that usually backfires.

To make matters worse, says Dr. Keith, television acts to limit people's physical activity, and to inundate adults and children alike with images of junk food and fast food.

In a study presented last year [2001] by the University of Chicago Children's Hospital, researchers revealed that black prime time television actually contains 60 percent more food and beverage commercials, and more images of soda and candy than are shown on general prime time television. Fully 36 percent of commercials during black prime time television, for instance, advertised desserts and sweets, while another 31 percent advertised fast food.

Constrained Choices

Members of disadvantaged groups understand that poverty constrains choices, including "life style" choices about what to eat. Limits of time and money, and habits learned at an early age, condemn many poor Americans to an excessively generous diet of processed and fast food. Perhaps "comfort food" is not misnamed. The distribution of obesity by income is similar to the distribution of tobacco use in the population—greater prevalence with lower income, as well as racial disparities.

Anthony Robbins, Wendy E. Parmet, and Richard Daynard, *Poverty & Race*, May/June 2003.

Most surprising was the finding that 27 percent of actors on black prime time were overweight, as opposed to only 2 percent on general prime time. According to the researchers, the prevalence of overweight characters on black prime time may be sending the detrimental message that obesity is acceptable, despite the attendant health risks.

But on another level, the presence of heavier actors on television may not, in and of itself, be a bad thing. In many communities of color, what constitutes a desirable or beautiful appearance is not always dictated by the narrow aesthetics of the dominant society.

In the African American community, celebrities including Oprah, Missy Elliott, Queen Latifah, India Arie, and Star Jones have played a part in helping many women of color to feel good about the way they look and to feel proud of their own generous curves.

The realization that health can be attained without shrinking one's natural body size is one of the most important messages that Gauthier tries to get across to her patients.

"What we need to focus on more than an unrealistic view

of what a woman's body should look like is that women are dying at alarming rates from obesity-related illnesses."

Rising Diabetes

Top among that list of illnesses is diabetes, which has struck communities of color particularly heavily.

"In our population, we're definitely seeing an increase in obese and diabetic patients," explains Camaro of La Clinica de la Raza. "Where we used to see people with Type 2 (non-insulin-dependent) diabetes after 40, we now have diabetics as young as 18 years of age."

Studies have confirmed that immigrants often fare worse in terms of their diet and weight after they leave their native countries. A large-scale 1998 University of North Carolina at Chapel Hill study demonstrated that adolescent obesity increases significantly among second and third-generation immigrants to the U.S.

In the study, all Asian immigrant groups except Chinese and Filipinos doubled their proportion of obese children during the transition from first to second generation residency. Latinos showed similar increases in obesity between first and second generations.

Other studies have shown that the prevalence of diabetes in Chinese Americans is reported to be five to seven times higher than the rates in China.

Perhaps no single ethnic group has been more devastated by obesity and diabetes than Native Americans, for whom the death rate from diabetes is nearly 250 percent greater than the national average.

On South Dakota reservations, including Rosebud and Pine Ridge, it's estimated that 50 to 60 percent of adults over 45 have diabetes. Children as young as 13 and 14 are being diagnosed with Type 2 diabetes, formerly called "adult-onset diabetes."

The nation's most extensively researched Native American tribe, the Pima Indians of Arizona, have even lent their bodies to science for the past three decades to help researchers prove the causal link between obesity and diabetes.

Among Pimas over the age of 55, 80 percent have diabetes. Amputations, blindness, and dialysis are now a regular part of Pima reservation life.

The extent of the research and the lack of direct health benefit to Pimas themselves have been criticized in recent years by community leaders, who point to the ever-growing rates of obesity and diabetes among Pima Indians as evidence of the fact that the research has helped scientists, but not the people being studied.

Body of Tradition

But one thing of use to health educators and physicians working with Native Americans has been the recognition that genetic factors have played a strong part in the prevalence of obesity and diabetes.

The so-called "thrifty gene" theory is based on the fact that, for thousands of years, many Indian tribes practiced an active hunting and gathering lifestyle, experiencing alternating periods of feast and famine. Their bodies evolved to allow them to store fat during "feast" times, so as to prevent starvation during leaner times.

Anthropological studies have suggested that 17 percent of 19th century Indians' caloric intake was from fat. Today, that figure is closer to 38 percent, as root vegetables, fish, buffalo, and berries have given way to soda pop, processed meats, dairy products, and a starch-heavy diet.

The U.S. government bears some direct responsibility for that dietary shift, notes Rogers of the Native Wellness Institute, in the form of the commodities provided to Indians on the reservation.

"I can remember being seven or eight and going with my grandparents to the Department of Agriculture in town and picking up our flour, cheese, and bucket of lard," says Rogers.

Unlike many of his young Indian peers, Rogers' Kiowa grandparents believed in serving more traditional foods, including berries, deer, and fish. His grandparents also inculcated in Rogers the importance of a respectful relationship to the creatures and environment that helped to sustain him.

But in the present-day, Rogers sees that physical wellness is suffering as a direct result of cultural, regional, and spiritual displacement among many Indian people.

"A lot of the reasons why people overeat or are obese is related to something deeper inside," says Rogers firmly. "Much of it is related to how much power we see ourselves as having. And part of where we are as a physical nation is directly related to our own acculturation, stress, and the problems we've had adapting to a society that we're not very comfortable with. So many of the problems in terms of obesity are related to pain and historical suffering."

"Traditionally, we've taken great pride in our bodies," Rogers adds. "Our bodies were viewed as [the vessel] carrying our spirit. And we have to treat our bodies with respect."

Periodical Bibliography

The following articles have been selected to supplement the diverse views presented in this chapter.

Radley Balko   "The 'War' Against Obesity," *National Post*, June 16, 2004.

Jane E. Brody   "Fat but Fit: A Myth About Obesity Is Slowly Being Debunked," *New York Times*, October 24, 2000.

Ellen Goodman   "Fit and Fat at the Same Time," *Liberal Opinion Week*, April 8, 2002.

Denise Grady   "Diabetes Rises; Doctors Foresee a Harsh Impact," *New York Times*, September 24, 2000.

Gina Kolata   "While Children Grow Fatter, Experts Search for Solutions," *New York Times*, October 19, 2000.

Michael Leahy   "The Fat of the Land: Americans' Love Affair with Food Comes with a Painful Cost for Too Many," *Washington Post*, August 16–22, 2004.

Rosie Mestrel   "Obesity Gaining on Tobacco as Top Killer," *Los Angeles Times*, March 10, 2004.

Rosie Mestrel   "Worth Its Weight in Debate," *Los Angeles Times*, July 23, 2004.

Cathy Newman   "Why Are We So Fat?" *National Geographic*, August 2004.

Randal O'Toole   "How Fat Are We?" *Liberty*, November 2002.

Neal Pierce   "Obesity Problems Worsen but Solutions Emerge," *Liberal Opinion Week*, July 12, 2004.

Anthony Robbins,   "Race, Poverty, and New Strategies to Control
Wendy E. Parmet,   the Obesity Epidemic," *Poverty & Race*,
and Richard Daynard   May/June 2003.

Joan Ryan   "In Fat Race, U.S. Leads, World Gains," *Liberal Opinion Week*, April 5, 2004.

William Skidelsky   "Food: Did You Know That Brad Pitt Is Overweight, and George Clooney Obese?" *New Statesman*, June 7, 2004.

Sally Squires   "We're Fat and Getting Fatter," *Washington Post*, October 14–20, 2002.

CHAPTER 2

What Causes Obesity?

Chapter Preface

Throughout the latter half of the twentieth century, two things have increased steadily in countries all over the world: television viewing by children and child obesity. This trend is especially pronounced in the United States, where child obesity rates and television viewing hours have both skyrocketed. A typical child in the United States now watches television for almost three hours every day, and approximately 15 percent of U.S. children are overweight. As experts explore why people are getting fatter in many areas of the world, child obesity garners especially intense interest.

The correlation between television watching and obesity has led many researchers to examine television viewing as a possible cause of obesity in children. Numerous studies confirm this connection. According to the *Lancet*, there are now over fifty published studies showing an association between television viewing and obesity in children. For example, in a 2001 study of over four thousand U.S. children, researchers found that as hours of television increased, prevalence of obesity rose. According to the study, obesity rates were lowest among children who watched an hour or less of television per day. In a 2001 article in the *Archives of Pediatric & Adolescent Medicine*, the authors conclude that "a few hours of TV are far from harmless."

While the connection between television watching and child obesity seems clear, the reasons for the connection are not clearly understood. Many researchers argue that television viewing results in obesity because it reduces physical activity among children. According to William Dietz, director of the Division of Nutrition and Physical Activity at the Centers for Disease Control, "Almost anything else uses more energy than watching TV." The TV-Turnoff Network, an organization that encourages children to watch less television, agrees with this position. In a 2001 article the organization claims that "there is no waking activity that we do that burns fewer calories than watching TV—a body in front of the tube is a body at rest."

Other commentators contend that television causes obesity because it exposes children to constant food advertisements urging them to eat. In the *Texas Daily Sentinel* journalist Elizabeth Lee writes, "It's no surprise that children who watch a lot of TV are more likely to be overweight than those who don't. But that may not be because they're glued to the tube instead of playing soccer." In her opinion, "A barrage of commercials for junk food is most likely the cause." According to a report from the Kaiser Family Foundation, a nonprofit group that studies health care issues, children see forty thousand commercials each year, double what they watched a generation ago. Most are for cereals, candy, and fast food. "Ten billion dollars in food industry advertising aimed at kids is a powerful counterweight to parents trying to get their kids to eat a balanced diet," says Vicky Rideout, a Kaiser vice president.

As obesity rates increase, especially among children, researchers, policy makers, and the general public have become increasingly concerned about the causes of obesity. The following chapter presents some of the latest views on why people in America and other parts of the world are getting fatter.

| *"The primary reason America is fat is that we eat too much compared to our activity level."*

Overeating and Lack of Exercise Cause Obesity

Amanda Spake and Mary Brophy Marcus

In the following viewpoint Amanda Spake and Mary Brophy Marcus maintain that the primary cause of obesity is the consumption of too many calories paired with a lack of exercise. Technological and social changes have reduced the need for physical activity, the authors point out, while at the same time provided a cheap and plentiful food supply. This combination, they argue, means that many people eat far more calories than their bodies burn, resulting in obesity. Spake and Marcus are contributing writers for *U.S. News & World Report*, a weekly magazine that offers analysis of world events.

As you read, consider the following questions:

1. In the authors' opinion, what driving force of human biology do most people act on?
2. How much sugar does the average American consume each day, according to Spake and Marcus?
3. What happened when Katie Young limited her food and increased her exercise, as explained by the authors?

Amanda Spake and Mary Brophy Marcus, "A Fat Nation," *U.S. News & World Report*, August 19, 2002. Copyright © 2002 by U.S. News & World Report, L.P. All rights reserved. Reproduced by permission.

Pretty, dark-haired Katie Young has been successful at most things. She's a nearly straight-A student, a big hitter on her softball team, and a good dancer. But like so many Americans—kids and adults alike—the New Orleans 10-year-old struggles with one thing: keeping her weight under control.

When Katie started day camp in June [2001], she discovered a snack bar where she could buy pizza, hot dogs, candy, ice cream, chips, soft drinks, and more. "Katie went nuts," says her mother, Judy Young. In the first two weeks of camp, Katie stole nearly $40 from her mother's purse for snack foods. "I bought a lot of pizza," Katie says. "It's good, of course, because it's from Pizza Hut. And I bought candy and everything. I didn't feel good seeing the other kids eat those things. I wanted them too."

Of course she did. Katie was acting on a basic driving force of human biology: Eat whenever food is available and eat as much of it as possible. Throughout most of human history, food was scarce, and getting ahold of it required a great deal of physical energy. Those who ate as many calories as they could were protected against famine and had the energy to reproduce. "As a result, humans are hard-wired to prefer rich diets, high in fat, sugar, and variety," says Kelly Brownell, director of the Yale Center for Eating and Weight Disorders. The problem today, Brownell adds, is that there's "a complete mismatch" between biology and the environment. Or as University of Colorado nutrition researcher James Hill puts it, "Our physiology tells us to eat whenever food is available. And now, food is always available." . . .

Too Much Food

Obesity has been linked to everything from the decline of the family dinner to the popularity of computers and video games to supersize portions of fast food. But it all comes down to a simple calculation, says Colorado's Hill: "The primary reason America is fat is that we eat too much compared to our activity level."

Over the past 50 years, as technology has reduced movement in daily life, the American diet has also changed, paralleling a revolution in food production. "The energy intensity of the human diet is going up," says Barry Popkin, a professor of nutrition at the University of North Carolina [UNC]–Chapel Hill. Human beings are eating more calories per bite than their ancestors ate. "The most common changes," Popkin explains, "are the added sugar in processed food and the added fat."

Before World War II, food was grown on small family farms and sold to local stores. Changes in farming practices resulted in an abundance of food, and innovations in processing, packaging, preservation, and refrigeration allowed products to be transported across continents. Companies made use of the new technology to produce a previously unimagined variety of processed and packaged foods and beverages. Today, a dozen or so food giants—so-called Big Food—produce, distribute, and sell much of what the world eats.

Without question the food industry has delivered something unique in human history: a dependable, low-cost food supply. "But now, food is so overproduced in the U.S. that there are 3,800 calories per person per day, and we only need about half of that," says Marion Nestle, chair of the Department of Nutrition and Food Studies at New York University. Judy Putnam, who studies food and nutritional patterns for the U.S. Department of Agriculture, agrees. USDA food-supply data show a 500-calorie-per-person daily increase between 1984 and 2000. Similarly, the USDA's dietary intake surveys show a 236-calorie-per-person-per-day increase between 1987 and 1995. Even that smaller estimate translates into an average 24-pound weight gain per person every year. Putnam figures that about 39 percent of the increase comes from refined grains, 32 percent from added fats, and 24 percent from more sugar.

Hard to believe, but Americans consume the equivalent of 20 to 33 teaspoons of sugar per person per day. About 30 percent of it is in soft drinks, but sugar is also the No. 1 additive. It is found in a variety of foods, says Putnam: "It turns up in some unlikely places, such as pizza, bread, hot dogs, soup, crackers, spaghetti sauce, lunchmeat, canned vegetables, fruit drinks, flavored yogurt, ketchup, salad dressing, and mayonnaise."

Greater use of prepared foods may have increased calories, but so has another major cultural change: eating out. Restaurant meals generally contain more fat, including more saturated fat, less fiber, more cholesterol, and more calories than homemade meals. In 1977–78, Americans ate about 19 percent of their total calories out. By 1995, they were eating 34 percent of their calories away from home. "The size of this increase is enormous," says UNC's Popkin, who analyzes the USDA's dietary surveys. "There has been a more than doubling of the calories consumed at restaurants and fast-food establishments over the past two decades."

That's in part because when people do eat out, they eat more. . . .

Courted by Food

Eating opportunities are endless because food is sold almost everywhere. "Just go back 20 years," says Yale's Brownell. "You never used to find more than a candy counter in a drugstore. Now there are aisles and aisles of food. If you see a gas station that does not have a food store attached, people are afraid to use it. There are food courts in shopping malls. And in the schools, there are vending machines and soft-drink machines—and they aren't selling carrot juice." . . .

There seems to be little connection between people's understanding of food availability and eating behavior and an awareness of their expanding waistlines. In an American Institute for Cancer Research survey in 2000, more than 3 in 4 of those polled said that the kind of food they ate was more important in maintaining or losing weight than the amount of food. Americans' false hope that calories don't count may explain a general ignorance about how much people are actually eating. In that same survey, 62 percent said that compared to 10 years ago restaurant portions are the same size or smaller. Few said they measured out food portions when they eat, nor could most correctly estimate a "serving" of pasta based on the USDA's portion guidelines. Not surprisingly, a sizable majority said they were overweight. Likewise, in a Harvard University survey released in May 2002, more than half of those surveyed said they were overweight. But 78 percent did not think their weight was a problem. Though the vast majority regarded cancer, AIDS, and heart disease as serious health problems, only a third thought obesity was.

One reason Americans are so clueless about weight may be because they still see obesity as an individual moral failing, not an environmental one. In the Harvard survey, 2 out of 3 people said the obesity epidemic could be explained by overweight people "lacking willpower" to diet and exercise. This is nonsense, says Colorado's Hill, who has studied more than 3,000 individuals who have successfully lost and maintained their weight loss. "The way society is today, the only way most people can maintain a healthy weight is with active cognitive control—that is, they are thinking about it most of the time." The problem, he adds, is that few people have the skills necessary to balance how much they're eating against the calories they're using up in physical activity.

A Changing Workplace

The nature of the American workplace may . . . be contributing to higher caloric intake. Whether people dine while sitting down at a table or while standing at a fast-food counter, at the workplace they are literally sitting down on the job more than they did during prior eras. More sedentary desk jobs probably contribute to wider bottoms. Consider two middle-income jobs, one in 1953 and one in 2003. In 1953, a dockworker lifts 50 boxes off of a minicrane and places it on a hand truck, which the dockworker pulls to a warehouse. In 2003, a person earning a similar income would be sitting in front of a computer, inputting data, and matching orders with deliveries.

What's the key difference? Until recently, employers paid employees to exert energy and burn calories. In contrast, [now] employers pay workers to stay in their seats. For many, the most vigorous exercise comes from tearing off a sheet of paper from a printer or walking to the refrigerator. Furthermore, I would suggest that the decline in factory work—with its fixed lunch and coffee break schedule—enables people to eat more often.

Todd G. Buchholz, *Journal of Controversial Medical Claims*, November 2003.

Obesity experts say that these skills need to be part of health education in schools. They're taught in many obesity-treatment programs—but those are generally out of reach for most Americans because they're not covered by health insurance. "Insurance coverage is a major obstacle to dealing with obesity," says Yale's Brownell. "The consequences of obesity, such as diabetes, get covered, but obesity [treatment] does not."

Cheap and Easy

In many ways, the Young family's struggle with weight typifies the causes of obesity and the challenges of dealing with it: Judy Young is a professional in the computer business, who says her job requires "sitting all the time in front of a computer screen." She's a single mother, and at night, exhausted with a hungry child to feed, the temptation to run to a fast-food restaurant for dinner is often too powerful to resist. "They make it so easy for you to 'biggie size' everything," Young says. She never thought fast food was a good choice, but it saved time for her to help Katie with her homework.

For several years, Katie bought breakfast and lunch at school. "They were so inexpensive," Young recalls. School breakfasts cost only 50 cents and offered doughnuts. Lunch was 65 cents, typically for pizza or a hot dog. Young knew her daughter needed more exercise, particularly after physical education at school was cut to one day a week. But she was nervous about letting Katie walk to school. "We live in a big city," she says, "and it just isn't safe."

By the time Katie was 7, she weighed nearly 130 pounds, about twice the normal body weight for her height and age. "I'm extremely obese, morbidly obese," says Young. "I'm diabetic. I have hypertension, and I saw my daughter moving in the same direction. I knew I had to do something." Young's health insurance plan refused to pay for obesity treatment for Katie and would cover only a minimal number of lab tests. Young borrowed the $2,500 to sign the family up for a childhood obesity treatment program at Louisiana State University called Committed to Kids.

The brainchild of an exercise physiologist, a nutritionist, and a psychologist from the Pennington Biomedical Research Center at LSU [Louisiana State University], the program focuses on lifestyle change, not dieting. It encourages eating lots of fruits and vegetables, limiting portion sizes, having no snack foods or sweets at home, and setting realistic goals for limiting food and increasing exercise. Katie has successfully lost 26 pounds, and she has also grown taller and added muscle, but she still has about 20 more pounds to lose.

In a few weeks Katie begins the school year, a difficult time for weight control. "Kids spend 48 percent of their waking hours in school and three hours a night on homework," says LSU's Melinda Sothern, a founder of Committed to Kids. "It's too much sitting. Homework is the No. 1 reason parents and kids say they can't fit exercise into their day."

The combination of homework and television can be a toxic one for kids like Katie. A large number of studies document that the incidence of obesity is lowest among children who watch one hour a day of television or less and greatest for those who watch four or more. A study published in *Pediatrics* in June [2002] showed that 40 percent of 1-to-5-year-olds had a television set in their bedrooms. Even among active preschoolers, those who watched more were more likely to be overweight. . . .

Where Do We Go from Here?

There are many proposals on the table, from lawsuits to junk-food taxes, school-based efforts to low-cost "fast health food" chains. . . .

It may be that healthful eating and physical activity can be marketed with the same tools used to sell burgers and fries. Since fewer than 10 percent of schools now offer daily physical education, last month [July 2002] the CDC [Centers for Disease Control and Prevention] began a $190 million multimedia campaign—called VERB—to get kids moving. Similarly, Margo Wootan, at the Center for Science in the Public Interest [CSPI], and Bill Reger, a medical professor at West Virginia University, waged a "1% or Less" campaign to persuade people to use low-fat milk. After eight weeks of paid advertising and a PR blitz, as many as 38 percent of high-fat drinkers in four West Virginia communities switched to low-fat milk. The campaign cost a little more than the equivalent of five coronary bypass operations, yet it reduced dietary saturated fat—and heart risk—for an estimated 30,540 people. Reger is developing a "Five a Day" antiobesity campaign emphasizing fruits and vegetables.

To make the public more calorie-conscious when dining out, health advocates want chain and fast-food restaurants to list the calorie content of their meals prominently on menus and food wrappers. "It wouldn't cost anything," says Michael Jacobson, director of CSPI, who first proposed this idea, "but it could have a major effect on food choices."

These and other obesity-prevention ideas could slim our collective paunch. But for some people, like Judy Young, the benefits won't come soon enough. "I've been on the liquid diet, [weight-loss drugs] fen-phen, Redux. I tried Atkins and the Zone [diets]" she says. Nothing lasted. This fall, Young plans to undergo gastric bypass surgery, a procedure in which the stomach is sectioned off and a small pouch is created, reducing the amount of food one can eat. Gastric bypass is only recommended for people who are 100 pounds or more overweight. Weight loss is rapid, but high rates of complications are associated with the surgery, and as many as 2 in 100 patients die from it.

Young knows these risks. She says she has weighed them again and again. "If I don't do it," she says, "I don't think I will live to see Katie grow up."

"The biggest myth about fat people is that they're gluttons."

There Is No Evidence That Overeating and Lack of Exercise Cause Obesity

Sandy Szwarc

While it is commonly believed that obesity is caused by eating too much and exercising too little, there is no scientific evidence to support this idea, argues Sandy Szwarc in the following viewpoint. According to Szwarc, clinical studies have repeatedly shown no difference between the diets and exercise patterns of fat and thin people. Thus, she concludes, there is no basis for claiming that the number of calories consumed and physical activity level are related to obesity. Szwarc is the author of hundreds of articles on nutrition, preventative health, and food. She is also the recipient of the 2004 Bert Greene Food Journalism Award.

As you read, consider the following questions:
1. According to Szwarc, how do the portion sizes of meals prepared at home compare with those served at fast-food restaurants?
2. In the author's opinion, how successful are diets as a weight loss strategy?
3. As explained by Szwarc, what did a 1996 American Heart Association study show about the correlation between weight and watching television?

S ome foods are so dangerously delicious that we must be protected from them and from ourselves—or so the thinking goes among certain trial lawyers, legislators, special-interest groups and the Health and Human Services secretary.

Myths About Obesity

These dietary watchdogs blame the obesity epidemic on fattening foods and the restaurants and food makers who tempt us with them. Fast-food restaurants especially must be stopped because they prey upon the poor and uneducated, duping them into ordering their greasy burgers and fries.

Declaring most of us too fat, they've proposed an assortment of punitive taxes, restrictive regulations and lawsuits to keep American appetites in check. But behind these ideas is an intrinsic prejudice against fat people as irresponsible, stupid gluttons who eat too much, especially too much of the "wrong" foods. Fat people are also seen as lazy slugs who do little exercise other than lifting the food from their plates to their mouths.

Lack of Evidence

In our thin-obsessed culture, such beliefs about the obese and manufactured foods abound, but these myths don't hold up to the evidence. Fast-food meals, for example, contain fewer calories from fat today [2004] than they did in the 1970s. And, in spite of their convenience, we still eat 75 percent of our meals at home, where portion sizes are even larger than those at fast-food restaurants, according to a recent U.S. Chamber of Commerce report.

In actuality, there is no scientific evidence that any specific food causes obesity.

A bill just introduced in the Senate could protect the food industry from predatory class-action lawsuits holding them liable for people's obesity.[1]

But it's doubtful that fat people will get off so easily. The truths about them are harder to accept.

1. In March 2004 the House of Representatives passed the Personal Responsibility in Food Consumption Act, intended to prevent frivolous lawsuits against the food industry.

Fat People Are Not Gluttons

The biggest myth about fat people is that they're gluttons. Yet in repeated clinical studies, researchers have found no meaningful difference in how many calories or the types of foods fat people eat compared with thinner people. That's counterintuitive, but true.

The Healthy Eating Index—the report card on how Americans eat, compiled by the U.S. Department of Agriculture—found in 1998 that those with ideal Hollywood figures ate a similar number of calories as those considered obese.

The Obese Speak Out About Obesity

A message to co-workers:
We the obese are not slobs
We the obese are not dirty
We the obese do not stink
We the obese are not stupid
We the obese do not eat everything that comes into reach
We the obese DO enjoy playing physical games
We the obese DO make good friends
We the obese DO try to fit in
We the obese DO care.　　　—*Tara (Beaverton, OR)* . . .

Persons who are morbidly obese are not lazy individuals who spend their days on the couch in front of the television with a box of cookies, a bag of chips, and a soft drink. We are mothers, fathers, professionals, educators, and community leaders. We are not substandard citizens. We do not like being obese. We have a disease. All we ask for is your respect as a colleague. Our weight is not a reflection of our professional abilities. Don't tease us about what and when we eat. If we ask for your encouragement, then do so tactfully. If we don't, then mind your own business.　　　—*Joe (Montgomery, AL)*

www.obesityhelp.com, 2003.

In fact, multiple studies have found that women who dutifully watch what they eat and are dainty eaters, or who diet, actually weigh more than those who don't restrict their food intake. In a 1990 study published in the American Journal of Clinical Nutrition, women controlling their eating had slowed their metabolisms down to where they were eating 410 fewer calories a day than their more slender but unrestrained eating friends.

The adage "diets don't work" is more accurately "diets make you fatter." The overwhelming body of scientific research has shown with striking consistency that less than 3 percent of weight loss is maintained over the long term.

That fact has played out on a national scale. Obesity rates soared throughout the mid-1960s to 1990, while we were eating steadily fewer calories and less fat, according to the Center for Nutrition Policy.

Fat People Are Not Sloths

Centers for Disease Control data also show that through the 1990s, exercise activity remained unchanged and, by some studies, increased.

That shatters the next myth: that fat people are necessarily sloths. Even the American Heart Association admitted in 1996 that studies looking at sedentary activity, particularly watching television, had found no differences between fat and slim youth.

Misplaced Blame

What did grow during those decades was our national preoccupation with thinness and the number of us dieting. Obesity is far too complicated and serious to look for lucrative food targets to blame.

Before we get behind policies and regulations to "fix" the obesity problem, we need to be sure they're based on sound science rather than intuition. Our favorite creme brulee may be at stake.

"Obesity is recognized as a disease in the U.S. and internationally by government, health organizations, researchers and medical professionals."

Obesity Is a Disease

American Obesity Association

In the following viewpoint the American Obesity Association argues that obesity is a disease and should be understood as such by the health care community and the general public. The association claims that obesity meets the dictionary definition of a disease because it has recognizable causes, has identifiable signs and symptoms, and results in consistent charges to the body. In addition, the association cites prominent health and government organizations that also believe obesity is a disease. The American Obesity Association is an organization focused on changing public policy and perceptions about obesity.

As you read, consider the following questions:

1. According to the association, what etiologic agents are associated with obesity?
2. As cited by the American Obesity Association, what results from the misconception that obesity is caused by a lack of willpower?
3. Why is obesity a remarkable disease, according to the National Academy of Sciences' Institute of Medicine?

The American Obesity Association (AOA) believes that obesity is a disease. We want obesity understood by the health care community and patients as a serious disease of epidemic portions.

Why do we think obesity is a disease?

First, let's define our terms. Dictionaries agree: obesity is excess body fat. It is not defined as a behavior. However, many people use the term obesity as short-hand for overeating or lack of exercise. But that is not its definition.

Consider this: most people can distinguish between smoking and lung cancer. One is a behavior and one is a disease. Or problem drinking of alcohol and liver disease. One is a behavior and one is a disease. Sunbathing without protection is a behavior; skin cancer is a disease.

Second, obesity—the excess accumulation of body fat—fits all the definitions of "disease." How is "disease" defined? Most dictionaries, general as well as medical, define a disease as an interruption, cessation or disorder of a bodily function, organ or system. Obesity certainly fits this definition.

Some dictionaries have a more precise definition. Stedman's Medical Dictionary says that to be a disease it should have at least two of the following three features:

- recognized etiologic agents
- identifiable signs and symptoms, and,
- consistent anatomical alterations.

The "recognized etiologic agents" for obesity include social, behavioral, cultural, physiological, metabolic and genetic factors.

The "identifiable signs and symptoms" of obesity include an excess accumulation of fat or adipose tissue, an increase in the size or number of fat cells, insulin resistance, increased glucose levels, increased blood pressure, elevated cholesterol and triglyceride levels, decreased levels of high-density lipoprotein and norepinephrine and alterations in the activity of the sympathetic and parasympathetic nervous system. One is also likely to find shortness of breath and back pain.

The "consistent anatomic alteration" of obesity is the increase in body mass. Therefore, obesity meets all three of the dictionary criteria for disease. . . .

Obesity is recognized as a disease in the U.S. and internationally by government, health organizations, researchers and medical professionals.

AOA and Shape Up America!

- The AOA and Shape Up America! collaborated to publish *Guidance for Treatment of Adult Obesity*, which states:

Obesity is a disease afflicting millions of Americans and causing a great deal of pain and suffering. Despite evidence to the contrary, many people view obesity as a lack of willpower on the part of the individual. As a result, obese persons are frequently the object of prejudice and discrimination.

National Institutes of Health (NIH)

- In a 1985 consensus statement [called] the *Health Implications of Obesity*, NIH declares:

Formerly, obesity was considered fully explained by the single adverse behavior of inappropriate eating in the setting of attractive foods. The study of animal models of obesity, biochemical alterations in man and experimental animals, and the complex interactions of psychosocial and cultural factors that create susceptibility to human obesity indicate that this disease in man is complex and deeply rooted in biologic systems. Thus, it is almost certain that obesity has multiple causes and that there are different types of obesity.

- The NIH's National Heart, Lung and Blood Institute's *Clinical Guidelines on the Identification, Evaluation, and Treatment of Overweight and Obesity in Adults*, state:

Obesity is a complex, multifactorial chronic disease that develops from an interaction of genotype and the environment. Our understanding of how and why obesity develops is incomplete, but involves the integration of social, behavioral, cultural, physiological, metabolic and genetic factors.

National Academy of Sciences' Institute of Medicine

- The National Academy of Sciences' Institute of Medicine formed a committee to evaluate the treatment and prevention of obesity. In their report, *Weighing the Options*, the committee states:

These figures (regarding the prevalence of obesity) point to the fact that obesity is one of the most pervasive public health problems in this country, a complex, multifactorial disease of appetite regulation and energy metabolism involving genetics, physiology, biochemistry, and the neurosciences, as well as environmental, psychological, and cultural factors. Unfortunately, the lay public and health-care providers, as well as

Comparing Obesity to Other Diseases

Several barriers to the development of a more widely accepted understanding of obesity as a disease entity still exist. Foremost, is the view that a person's weight is determined by his or her will power and is thus exclusively a matter of personal responsibility. In this view the person who is overweight or obese is blamed for his or her condition and there is a judgement that support or assistance, which might be otherwise forthcoming, should be withheld. On the other hand, many persons have difficulty with the idea of disease as a condition that may be self-inflicted. In their view, disease is something that one acquires, like an infection or is predisposed to, as a result of genetics—not something over which a person has control. In this model of disease, the individual is a victim and blameless. . . . Human immunodeficiency virus (HIV)/acquired immunodeficiency syndrome (AIDS) and other sexually transmitted diseases may be brought about by risk-taking personal behavior to an even greater extent than the condition of obesity may be brought about; but they, too, are still regarded as diseases. Lung cancer may be preventable in many cases by lifestyle changes (e.g. smoking cessation), but it is regarded as a disease nonetheless. Injuries sustained by athletes such as mountain bikers or boxers, or injuries sustained by bungee jumpers or automobile drivers who drive without seat belts or while intoxicated, are all termed "accidents"; yet health insurance still covers the medical and hospital costs. . . .

In summary, obesity is a condition that fulfills all the reasonable definitions of a disease and major medical authorities now recognize obesity as a disease entity. A continuing effort to educate the public to the fact that obesity is a long-term chronic disease is required to overcome the misinformation and stigma commonly associated with this life-threatening condition.

Morgan Downey, *American Heart Journal*, December 2001.

insurance companies, often view it simply as a problem of willful misconduct—eating too much and exercising too little. Obesity is a remarkable disease in terms of the effort required by an individual for its management and the extent of discrimination its victims suffer.

Federal Trade Commission (FTC)
• The Partnership for Healthy Weight Management, a coalition of organizations led by the FTC developed

Voluntary Guidelines for Providers of Weight Loss Products or Services. The Partnership states:

"Obesity is a serious, chronic disease that is known to reduce life span, increase disability and lead to many serious illnesses including diabetes, heart disease, and stroke." The guidelines were established to "promote sound guidance to the general public on strategies for achieving and maintaining a healthy weight."

Maternal and Child Health Bureau

- An expert committee was formed by the Maternal and Child Health Bureau, a branch of the U.S. Department of Health and Human Services, at a March, 1997 conference on obesity in children and adolescents. Committee members were chosen for their clinical and research experience in the field of pediatric obesity to develop guidance on assessment and treatment for physicians, nurse practitioners, dietitians/nutritionists, and others who care for overweight children. The committee stated,

"Obesity represents a chronic disease," and "obesity in children and adolescents represents one of the most frustrating and difficult diseases to treat."

World Health Organization (WHO)

- A WHO Consultation on Obesity reported:

Obesity is a chronic disease, prevalent in both developed and developing countries, and affecting children as well as adults. Indeed it is so common that it is replacing the more traditional public health concerns, including undernutrition and infectious diseases, as one of the most significant contributors to ill health.

The WHO publishes the International Classification of Diseases (ICD-9-CM), which lists Obesity and Other Hyperalimentation as an Endocrine, Nutritional, Metabolic and Immunity Disease. The ICD-9-CM is recommended for use in all clinical settings, and is required for reporting diagnoses and diseases to all U.S. Public Health Service and Health Care Financing Administration programs. . . .

American Heart Association (AHA)

- In June 1998, the AHA added obesity to the association's list of major risk factors that people can control to prevent death and disability from coronary heart disease,

the cause of heart attacks. Other major risk factors include smoking, high blood cholesterol, high blood pressure, sedentary lifestyle. According to Robert H. Eckel,
M.D., vice chairman of the AHA's Nutrition Committee:

Obesity itself has become a life-long disease, not a cosmetic
issue, nor a moral judgement—and it is becoming a dangerous epidemic.

American Academy of Family Physicians (AAFP)

• The AAFP Congress, the Academy's policy-making
  body, adopted a policy on obesity stating:

The AAFP recognizes obesity as a disease and a national
health risk for premature death; will support CME [Contin-
uing Medical Education] programs on childhood obesity;
and promotes nutritionally balanced meals, decreased TV
viewing and increased physical activities for obese children.

American Society for Bariatric Surgery (ASBS)

• The ASBS states in their *Rationale for the Surgical Treatment of Morbid Obesity:*

The physiologic, biochemical and genetic evidence is overwhelming that clinically morbid obesity is a complex disorder.

The American Society of Bariatric Physicians (ASBP)

• ASBP states in their Frequently Asked Questions:

Recognized since 1985 as a chronic disease, obesity is the
second leading cause of preventable death, exceeded only by
cigarette smoking. Obesity has been established as a major
risk factor for hypertension, cardiovascular disease, diabetes
mellitus and some cancers in both men and women.

> *"Obesity is the result of . . . gluttony and sloth. Classifying obesity as a disease flies in the face of this rather obvious, though unpopular, understanding."*

Obesity Is Not a Disease

George Hawley

Obesity results from lack of self-control, asserts George Hawley in the following viewpoint. Whereas a disease is something people have no control over, he argues, individuals can make the choice to gain or lose weight. Hawley is opposed to the classification of obesity as a disease because he believes such a designation will stop people from taking personal responsibility for being overweight. Hawley is a research associate at the Center for Individual Freedom, a nonprofit organization that strives to protect and defend individual freedoms.

As you read, consider the following questions:

1. In Hawley's opinion, how is the classification of obesity as a disease an "ominous intrusion into all our lives"?
2. What two deadly sins does obesity result from, according to the author?
3. As argued by Hawley, how does using tax dollars to pay for obesity send the wrong message?

George Hawley, "Fattening Government, Slimming Choice," www.cfif.org, September 15, 2004. Copyright © 2004 by the Center for Individual Freedom. All rights reserved. Reproduced by permission.

E arlier this year [2004], the federal government discovered yet another crisis of catastrophic proportions—we're too fat. Bowing to incessant media coverage spurred on by those who continually insist that the "sky is falling," the U.S. government officially recognized that America is weighed-down in an "obesity crisis." And, what's more, we can't save ourselves, at least not without the help of those in Washington, or so they say.

Thus, through what seemed to be an innocuous observation, the federal government promised an ominous intrusion into all our lives. By recognizing obesity as a disease, the Feds took their first definitive steps toward inserting bureaucrats into individual decisions about what we eat and drink, assuring us that the federal government would help us change our "waist-full" ways.

Specifically, Medicare authorities announced in July [2004] that all language stating that obesity is not a disease would be removed from the Medicare coverage manual, thereby allowing Medicare payments for obesity treatments. With this change, Medicare will soon underwrite diet programs, behavioral counseling and stomach stapling.

Ignoring all of the pseudo-scientific research that tries to absolve overweight individuals from bearing any responsibility for their size, we should be specific about what obesity really is. Obesity is the inevitable consequence of eating too much and exercising too little. Although saying so violates the sacred tenets of political correctness, obesity is the result of two deadly sins: gluttony and sloth. Classifying obesity as a disease flies in the face of this rather obvious, though unpopular, understanding.

According to the American Heritage Dictionary, a disease is "a pathological condition of a part, organ, or system of an organism resulting from various causes, such as infection, genetic defect, or environmental stress, and characterized by an identifiable group of signs or symptoms." Using such a definition to account for obesity implies that an individual bears no responsibility for being overweight, as though obesity just randomly happens.

Nonsense.

Despite whatever ludicrous excuses the crusading special

interests and avaricious trial lawyers may come up with to shift the blame elsewhere, obesity is still a matter of self-control. No one is forced to eat more calories than they burn, and overweight people can see dramatic improvements in their health and appearance by changing their lifestyles.

A Definition That Does Not Make Sense

Obesity has been arbitrarily defined by the government as including anyone with a body mass index over 30, lumping about 20% of Americans into that category.

But millions of people, 25%–30% of the so-called obese people in the United States, have no health problems linked to weight.

Do we consider them diseased if they have no health problems? Some argue that they may develop health problems in the future, but I see many older people who are considered overweight but continue to live long lives. It is unfair to label all of these people as diseased when there is nothing medically wrong with them.

Glenn A. Gaesser, *Family Practice News*, August 15, 2003.

Nevertheless, the new talking points used in the obesity debate demonstrate just how far we have wandered from medical and scientific reality. Obesity is now dubbed an "epidemic," a contagion needful of containment. But being overweight is not like contracting the flu or the bubonic plague. It results from a lifetime of individual choices. And just because a large number of people choose to over-indulge and under-exert does not make those choices everyone else's fault.

Sending the Wrong Message

Using our tax dollars to pay for weight loss sends the wrong message loud and clear: "Obesity is not your fault. You cannot lose weight on your own, so we will spend whatever it takes to help you." If government picks up the tab for overeating, then for what will individuals be held accountable? Personal responsibility will be unnecessary, at the cost of individual freedom. After all, since obesity has been officially dubbed as too big for individuals to deal with on their own, Big Brother will undoubtedly come to our aid, every single one of us, limiting all our choices.

It is only a matter of time before the public health crusaders, trial lawyers and state governments facing budget shortfalls unleash their fury on "big food." And, if the assault on eating continues to mimic the attacks on asbestos, silicone breast implants, tobacco, then our right to eat and drink what we want will be eroded in a drive to advance what others believe is for "the common good." Quite simply, if government cannot convince Americans to eat healthy, it can force us to do so through new taxes and lawsuits.

Creating a Social Burden

Soon (if we aren't already) we will hear that the fast food chains addicted us to grease; that restaurants purposely marketed kid's meals to impressionable children; that cartoon characters made overeating "cool"; and that nutritional information was purposely withheld from the public. Trial lawyers are already arguing that overweight people are helpless victims of everyone's favorite whipping boy, corporate America, while aggressively seeking jackpot justice to stop the food industry from engaging in the unconscionable practice of giving American consumers exactly what they want.

As stated famously more than two centuries ago, free people have an unalienable right to make their own choices. But they will not stay free for long if they demand that others must bear the responsibility for their own decisions. Classifying obesity as a disease officially changes hedonism from an individual imperfection into a societal burden. As a result, our limited government will soon be intruding into yet another aspect of our private lives, and we will find ourselves with fewer choices to make and fewer ways to make them.

People eat in units. That is, if they are offered a food that comes in a preportioned unit, such as a cookie, most people will eat the whole cookie. One of the most common unit foods is the sandwich. In most fast-food establishments, there is a choice of sandwich sizes; often the larger sandwiches are purchased because they are perceived as being a better value because they offer more food per dollar. The key question is: if consumers choose a larger sandwich, are they likely to eat more either at that meal or throughout the entire day? To test this, on 4 different days we offered men and women submarine sandwiches that varied in size: 6, 8, 10, and 12 inches. We found a systematic and significant effect of portion size on intake for both men and women. When served the 12-inch sandwich compared to the 6-inch sandwich, women consumed 31% more energy and men consumed 56% more energy. Hunger and fullness ratings after lunch did not differ significantly when subjects were served the 8-, 10-, and 12-inch sandwiches, despite the increase in energy intake. When served bigger portions, consumers override or adjust their level of satiety to accommodate greater energy intakes.

The amount of food in a package or container may also influence how much is eaten. Certainly, some prepackaged foods come in several sizes. For example, bags of potato chips range from 1-ounce (28 g) single-serving bags to 20-ounce (560 g) family-size bags. To test how the size of the bag affects intake, on 5 different occasions we served men and women an afternoon snack that consisted of 28, 42, 85, 128, or 170 g of potato chips in a plain unlabeled foil bag. Participants ate directly from the bag so that they had few visual cues to guide consumption. The results showed that portion size had a significant effect on snack intake for both the men and the women. Many individuals ate all of the chips in the two smaller bags, but most did not consume all of the chips in the 85-g package. However, when they were served the 170-g package, women ate 18% more and men ate 37% more than when served the 85-g package. When dinner was served several hours later, participants did not adjust their intakes to compensate for the differences in snack intake. Thus, bigger portions of a prepackaged snack increased energy intake in the short-term. It is not clear that

"*There are enough data to suggest that large portions of energy-dense foods are contributing to the obesity epidemic.*"

Large Portion Sizes Play a Role in Rising Obesity Rates

Barbara J. Rolls

In the following viewpoint Barbara J. Rolls examines the relationship between food portion sizes in the United States and the country's rising rates of obesity. She finds that the food industry is offering consumers increasingly larger portions of calorie-dense foods, and that the availability of these large portions causes people to eat more than their bodies need. Rolls concludes that to avoid obesity, people must learn to balance their calorie consumption with their bodies' needs rather than just eat what is placed in front of them. Rolls holds the Helen A. Guthrie Chair in Nutrition in the Department of Nutritional Sciences at Pennsylvania State University.

As you read, consider the following questions:
1. What does the author mean when she says, "people eat in units"?
2. As explained by Rolls, how does package or container size affect how much food is eaten?
3. Large portions of which types of food should be encouraged, according to the author?

Barbara J. Rolls, "The Supersizing of America: Portion Size and the Obesity Epidemic," *Nutrition Today,* vol. 38, March/April 2003, p. 42. Copyright © 2003 by Lippincott/Williams & Wilkins. Reproduced by permission of the publisher and the author.

In the United States, an obesity epidemic is rapidly becoming the most challenging public health problem that we have faced as a nation. Despite the known health consequences, the prevalence of both overweight and obesity has continued to increase. The National Health and Nutrition Examination Surveys show that the percentage of adults who were overweight or obese increased from 55.9% in 1988 through 1994 to 64.5% in 1999 through 2000. During this same period, the percentage of overweight teenagers increased from 10.5% to 15.5%. It is unlikely that our biology has changed during this short time, so other explanations for this surge in obesity rates must be found.

Both food supply data (which give an estimate of energy availability per person) and large-scale dietary surveys indicate that US adults are eating more calories per day than they were in the late 1970s. . . . This article presents data that suggest that increasing portion sizes are contributing to the obesity epidemic. . . .

Supersizing: The Expanding Size of Portions

An obvious place to start in addressing the relationship between portion size and obesity is to ask whether increases in portion size have indeed occurred, and, if so, whether they coincide with the rise in obesity rates. It is critical, however, when considering such associations to remember that they do not prove causality. [Researchers Lisa R.] Young and [Marion] Nestle compared current portions of restaurant foods, grocery products, and recipes in cookbooks with comparable older data. They found a rise in portion size in all food categories except bread. The expansion of portions started in the 1970s, increased sharply in the 1980s, and has continued to rise. As portions have grown, they have become more dissociated from recommended serving sizes such as those in the Food Guide Pyramid and on food labels.

We are now surrounded by "huge food"; muffins can weigh half a pound, and pasta bowls in restaurants hold more than 2 pounds. A plate of steak or fish that weighs more than a pound is no longer unusual restaurant fare. In a movie house, a "medium" popcorn is 16 cups (with up to 1,000 calories), and the soft drink that accompanies it may contain 500

calories. Two recent analyses of nationally representa[tive] vey data find that the reported portion sizes consume[d] eral foods have increased between 1977 and 1998. O[f partic]ular interest was the finding that portion sizes increas[ed] outside and inside the home, with the largest increa[se] at fast-food establishments. This demonstration that [portion] sizes and obesity rates have increased in parallel, [although] not proving causality, supports the hypothesis that [portion] size could play a role in increasing body weights.

Studies Show That Portion Size Affects Int[ake]

In addition to the data showing that there is an as[sociation] between increasing portions and the prevalence [of over-]weight and obesity, recent controlled studies show[...] that portion size affects energy intake. When we te[sted how] adults responded to 4 different portions of maca[roni and] cheese served on different days, we found that the [larger the] portion, the more participants ate. The participa[nts con-]sumed 30% more energy when offered the larges[t portion] (1000 g) compared to the smallest portion (500 g)[. Particu-]larly interesting is that participants reported similar [levels of] hunger and fullness after eating despite the inta[ke differ-]ences. The results were not affected by subject char[acteristics] including gender, body mass index, or concern abou[t food in-]take or body weight. After the study, fewer than hal[f of] the subjects reported noticing that there were diff[erences in] the portions served. It is surprising that in a contro[lled labo-]ratory setting where the main focus was food a[nd eating,] many participants in the study were unaware of th[e increase] in the amount of food offered and the subsequen[t increase in] their intake, hunger, and satiety. It is likely that in [settings] where there are more distractions, such as when [eating out,] consumers would be even less aware of portion siz[e.]

It could be argued that the effects of portion s[ize on in-]take are specific to foods such as macaroni and c[heese that] are amorphous in shape. It is particularly difficu[lt to judge] the portion size of such foods, especially when th[e portions] are large. We conducted further studies to test w[hether in-]take is also influenced by the portion size of oth[er kinds of] foods, such as these with clearly defined shapes o[...]

all prepackaged foods have a similar effect. It is possible that the effect will be greatest for highly palatable foods, such as potato chips, that people find difficult to stop eating. It is also possible that the effect will be different in other situations, such as when the snack is poured into a bowl so that the consumer can more readily assess the amount.

Supersized Servings

Burger King	1954	2004
Hamburger	2.8 oz.	4.3 oz.
	202 calories	310 calories
McDonald's	1955	2004
French Fries	2.4 oz.	7 oz.
	210 calories	610 calories
Hershey's	1900	2004
Chocolate	2 oz.	7 oz.
Bar	297 calories	1000 calories
Coca-Cola	1916	2004
Soft Drink	6.5 fluid oz.	16 fluid oz.
	79 calories	194 calories
Movie Popcorn	1950s	2004
	3 cups	21 cups (buttered)
	174 calories	1,700 calories

Cathy Newman, *National Geographic*, August 2004.

Additional studies conducted in various situations confirm that the package or container size of several foods can affect how much food is prepared and eaten. When women were given a 2-pound box of spaghetti and asked to take out enough to make a dinner for two, they removed an average of 302 strands. But when given a one-pound box, they removed only 234 strands. When frying chicken, women poured 4.3 ounces of cooking oil from a 32-ounce bottle, but only 3.5 ounces from a 16-ounce bottle. When people were asked how many M&Ms they would eat when watching a movie by themselves, participants poured 63 from a small package that contained 114 candies, 103 from a package double in size, and 122 from a package triple in size. That is, they poured about twice as much from a jumbo bag, a difference of approximately 250 calories. In a movie theater, consumers were given either a medium (120 g) or large (240 g) bucket of popcorn. Subjects rated the taste of the popcorn and were divided into two groups depending upon whether they perceived the taste as favorable or unfavorable. The results showed a large effect of the portion size of popcorn on intake in both groups. The larger package led to 49% more intake by those who rated the popcorn favorably (94 versus 63 g) and 61% more by those who rated the popcorn as relatively unfavorable (92 versus 57 g). Thus, it is not just the sensory attributes or the perceived pleasantness of foods that is driving intake when large portions are available. . . .

Eating Out and Portion Size

Although there is some evidence that portions consumed at home are increasing, the large portions served in restaurants may be a bigger problem for weight management. The increase in the prevalence of obesity since the 1970s coincides with an increase in the number of meals eaten outside the home. Studies show that in both adolescents and adults, the frequency of eating out is associated with an increase in energy and fat intake and with a higher body mass index. In particular, eating in fast-food restaurants is associated with increased energy intake and body fatness. When eating out, portion size is one of numerous variables that could affect consumption. Several palatable foods, a convivial atmosphere with friends, and alcohol consumption may also increase energy intake. In particular, the tendency to choose foods high in energy density (calories per gram) is likely to increase calorie intake, and these foods become particularly problematic when served in large portions.

Let us consider how the size of the portions offered in restaurants is determined. Although few published data are available, in one small study in Scotland of how caterers decide on portion sizes, the factors rated as most important were cost of the food, personal experience, and nutritional content. When caterers were asked what portions they would serve of several foods, the responses varied widely. For example, portions of rice varied from 80 to 380 g and French fries from 70 to 260 g. Clearly, customers should not rely on the restaurant to serve a portion that is related to their energy needs. Indeed, it is hard to imagine how this can be accomplished. Information is needed about the customer's body mass index, when he or she last ate, his or her activity level and metabolic rate, and how hungry he or she is. Because such "personalized portions" are unlikely to become a reality, we must consider other ways to manage portion size.

Value Meals

Restaurants have found that customers appreciate good value, and this translates into large portions at a low price. Because food is only a small percentage of the cost of a restaurant meal, giving customers more food is an excellent economic strategy if it increases total sales. Thus the practice of "supersizing," (giving customers a lot more food and calories for only a small additional cost) is widespread, particularly in fast-food establishments. For example, when ordering a cheeseburger, spending $1.57 more can buy 600 extra calories; for French fries, 64 cents can buy 330 more calories; and for some soft drinks, 37 cents can buy 450 more calories.

Restaurants may be giving consumers what they want in terms of value, but the crucial issue is whether people can adjust their energy intake to their energy needs when tempted with huge portions of energy-dense palatable foods. Faced with a lack of data in the scientific literature, the American Institute for Cancer Research commissioned several surveys examining consumers' perceptions of the portions they are served. The surveys found that 78% of the respondents believed that the type of food they eat is more important for weight management than the amount of food. Furthermore, 62% were unaware that portions served in restaurants have increased in size during the past 10 years. Regardless of the amount served, 67% said they finish their entrees most of the time or always. Many consumers are eating what is served, whether or not it is appropriate for their energy needs. . . .

I Ate It Because It Was There!

Clearly, consumers are responsible for what and how much they choose to eat. But several different studies show that people find it difficult to resist large portions and the ready availability of food. An interest in the way that portion size affects intake can be found as far back as 1957 when [researcher P.S.] Siegel published a short article titled The Completion Compulsion in Human Eating. He showed that young men eat foods in units. Thus, when a range of foods was preportioned into arbitrary units or servings, the men ate whole units rather than intermediate amounts. We observed this tendency in our study of varying sizes of submarine sandwiches, particularly when the men were eating the smaller sandwiches.

Perhaps related to this observation is the not-surprising finding that in some individuals there is a tendency to eat all the food put in front of them, or to "clean the plate." This was demonstrated in a study conducted in the late 1970s. Researchers served people soup from normal bowls to determine each person's customary intake. On the fourth day, without telling anyone, the researchers substituted a "trick bowl" that slowly refilled itself from a hidden reservoir under the table so that it was never empty. Regardless of whether the participants were obese or lean, the continual presence of food in the bowl stimulated them to eat more than their usual portion. After one day, the subjects were told about the trick, and their intake was then measured during the next 6 days. The normal-weight individuals adjusted their intake to baseline levels, whereas the participants who were obese continued to overeat, apparently unable to resist the food in the bowl. These data suggest that some individuals, when given information about the foods they are eating and appropriate portions, may adjust their intake and resist overeating in the face of the continual availability of food.

Other studies confirm that simply making food more readily available increases consumption. For example, in a large hospital cafeteria, when the lid was kept on an ice-cream cooler, only 3% of participants who were obese and 5% of normal-weight participants selected ice cream. But when the lid was taken off the cooler, allowing people to see the ice cream and reach it more easily, the percentages rose: 17% of the participants who were obese and 16% of the participants who were lean chose ice cream. In another recent study, the visibility and accessibility of chocolate candy was varied in workers' offices throughout 3 weeks. Both variables significantly affected the amount eaten: an average of 9 candies per person were consumed when the chocolate was visible on the desk, 6 were consumed when the candies were in a drawer of the desk, and only 3 were consumed when they were out of sight 2 m from the desk.

Fortunately, the principle of easy availability also works with foods low in energy density, such as soup and fruits. Simply stockpiling soup in the house can increase the frequency of soup consumption. Even the position of fruit in the house affects intake. In one study, people were asked to put fruit in the refrigerator, in a bowl in the kitchen, or in a bowl in the dining room. The participants ate the most fruit when it was in a bowl in the kitchen and the least when it was in the refrigerator.

Collectively, these studies show that we are responsive to environmental food cues. Whether or not we need food, when it is put in front of us, we eat. Many of us eat all of it. Physiologic satiety cues are readily overridden by food cues, such as large portions and the ready availability of food. The studies also suggest that it may be possible to decrease energy intake by structuring the environment so that large portions of foods low in energy density are readily available, while limiting the portion size and availability of foods higher in energy density. . . .

Urgent Action Needed

Although we are just beginning to understand how environmental factors, such as portion size, affect eating behavior, there are enough data to suggest that large portions of energy-dense foods are contributing to the obesity epidemic. Although it is not yet clear which will be the most effective strategies for bringing intake back in line with energy requirements, the continuing rise in the rates of obesity calls for urgent action. Interventions must be initiated and their efficacy monitored in several settings. The complexity of the issues involved—economic, political, psychologic, educational —demands cooperation among scientists and the public and the private sectors. Clearly, individuals bear the ultimate responsibility for how much they eat, but innovative initiatives to help them to resist our abundant environment could help to slow the obesity epidemic. Above all, when considering the influence of portion size, remember that it is not portion size that is the problem, but rather big portions of energy-dense foods that encourage excess energy intake. Large portions of foods low in energy density, such as fruits and vegetables, not only are acceptable but also should be encouraged.

"Evolving during a time of scarcity, humans developed an instinctive desire for basic tastes—sweet, fat, salt—that they could never fully satisfy."

Obesity Is a Result of Human Evolution

Michael D. Lemonick

In the following viewpoint Michael D. Lemonick claims that humans have a genetically based desire to eat whenever food is plentiful. Throughout most of human history, food was scarce, and intense physical exertion was required to obtain it. In response, humans evolved an innate desire to eat whenever they had the opportunity and to crave high-energy foods such as fats and sugars. While humans living in affluent nations now produce plentiful amounts of food with little physical effort, says Lemonick, people still possess that powerful drive to eat, resulting in constant overeating and obesity. Lemonick is an associate editor at *Time* magazine. He has contributed articles to the *Washington Post*, the *Sunday Times of London*, *Science '83*, and other publications.

As you read, consider the following questions:

1. According to Lemonick, where is the fat crisis most acute?
2. Why did it take constant work for our earliest ancestors to find enough food to stay alive, as explained by the author?
3. When did exercise begin to vanish from everyday life, according to Lemonick?

Michael D. Lemonick, "How We Grew So Big: Diet and Lack of Exercise Are Immediate Causes—But Our Problem Began in the Paleolithic Era," *Time International*, vol. 164, August 9, 2004. Copyright © 2004 by Time, Inc. All rights reserved. Reproduced by permission.

It's hardly news anymore that people are just too fat. If the endless parade of articles, TV specials and fad diet books weren't proof enough, a quick look around the shops, the beach or the crowd at any football match will leave no room for doubt: individual weight problems have become an international crisis.

Even so, the actual numbers are shocking. Fully two-thirds of U.S. adults are officially overweight, and about half of those have graduated to full-blown obesity. Among U.S. kids between 6 and 19 years old, 15% (or 1 in 6) are overweight, and another 15% are headed that way. In the European Union [E.U.], between 10% and 20% of men and 10% and 25% of women are obese, according to a survey carried out by the European Association for the Study of Obesity before the accession of 10 new members in May [2004]. Even pets are pudgy: a depressing 25% of U.S. dogs and cats are too heavy.

And things haven't been moving in a promising direction. Just two decades ago, the incidence of overweight U.S. adults was well under 50%, while the rate for kids was only a third what it is today. In the E.U. an estimated 18% of children are overweight or obese. People are clearly worried.

It wouldn't be such a big deal if the problem were simply aesthetic. But excess weight significantly increases the risk of heart disease, high blood pressure, stroke, diabetes, infertility, gall-bladder disease, osteoarthritis and many forms of cancer. The European Association for the Study of Obesity found that 8% of the healthcare costs in the E.U.—about 42 billion—go toward the treatment of obesity-related illnesses. The total medical tab in the U.S. for conditions related to obesity is $117 billion a year—and climbing—according to the Surgeon General. The *Journal of the American Medical Association* in the U.S. and a government health committee in the U.K. have both warned that obesity, exacerbated by a poor diet and physical inactivity, could soon overtake tobacco as the leading cause of preventable death.

So why is it happening? The obvious, almost trivial answer is that people eat too much high-calorie food and don't burn it off with enough exercise. Breaking those habits would make the problem go away. But clearly it isn't that easy. Consumers pour scores of billions of dollars every year into weight-loss products and health-club memberships and liposuction and gastric bypass operations—100,000 of the latter last year [2003] in the U.S. alone. Food and drug companies spend even more trying to find a magic food or drug that will melt the weight away. Yet the West's collective waistline just keeps expanding.

It's natural to try to find something to blame—fast-food joints or food manufacturers, or even the individual for having too little willpower. But the ultimate reason for obesity may be rooted deep within our genes. Obedient to the inexorable laws of evolution, the human race adapted over millions of years to living in a world of scarcity, where it paid to eat every good-tasting thing in sight when you could find it.

Although our physiology has stayed pretty much the same for the past 50,000 years or so, we humans have utterly transformed our environment. Over the past century especially, technology has almost completely removed physical exercise from the day-to-day lives of most people in the West. At the same time, it has filled supermarket shelves with cheap, mass-produced, good-tasting food that is packed with calories. And finally, technology has allowed advertisers to deliver constant, virtually irresistible messages that say "Eat this now" to everyone old enough to watch TV.

This artificial environment is most pervasive in the U.S. and other industrialized countries, and that's exactly where the fat crisis is most acute. When people move to the U.S. from poorer nations, their collective weight begins to rise. As developing areas like Southeast Asia and Latin America catch up economically and the inhabitants adopt Western lifestyles, their problems with obesity catch up as well. By contrast, among people who still live in conditions most like those of our distant Stone Age ancestors—such as the Maku or the Yanomami of Brazil—there is virtually no obesity at all.

And that's almost certainly the way it was during 99.9% of human evolution. For most of the 7 million years or so since we parted ways with chimps, life has been very harsh—"nasty, brutish and short," in [philosopher] Thomas Hobbes' memorable phrase. The average life expectancy was probably well under 30. But much of that dismal brevity can be chalked up to accidents, infections, traumatic childbirth and unfortunate encounters with saber-toothed cats and other such predators. If a Cro-Magnon, say, could get past these formidable obstacles, he might conceivably live into his 60s or even longer, with none of the obesity-related illnesses that plague people today.

Our earliest ancestors probably ate much as their cousins the apes did, foraging for fruits, shoots, nuts, tubers and other vegetation in the forests and savannas of Africa. Because most wild plants are relatively low in calories, it took constant work just to stay alive. Fruits, full of natural sugars like fructose and glucose, were an unusually concentrated source of energy, and the instinct to seek out and consume them evolved in many mammals long before humans ever arose. Fruit wasn't always available, but those who ate all they could whenever it was were more likely to survive and pass on their sweet tooth to their progeny.

Our love affair with sugar—and also with salt, another crucial but not always available part of the diet—goes back millions of years. But humanity's appetite for animal fat and protein is probably more recent. It was some 2.5 million years ago that our hominid ancestors developed a taste for meat. The fossil record shows that the human brain became markedly bigger and more complex about the same time. And indeed, according to Katherine Milton, an anthropologist at the University of California, Berkeley, "the incorporation of animal matter into the diet played an absolutely essential role in human evolution."

For starters, meat provided a concentrated source of protein, vitamins, minerals and fatty acids that helped our human ancestors grow taller. The first humans were the size of small chimps, but the bones of a Homo ergaster boy dating back about 1.5 million years suggest that he could have stood more than 1.8 m as an adult. Besides building our bodies, says Dr. S. Boyd Eaton of Emory University in Atlanta, the fatty acids found in animal-based foods would have served as a powerful raw material for the growth of human brains.

Because it's so packed with nutrients, meat gave early humans a respite from constant feeding. Like lions and tigers, they didn't have to eat around the clock just to keep going. But more important, unlike the big cats, which rely mostly on strength and speed to bring down dinner, our ancestors depended on guile, organization and the social and technological skills made possible by their increasingly complex brains. Those who were smartest about hunting—and about gathering the plant foods they ate as part of their omnivorous diets—tended to be better fed and healthier than the competition. They were thus more likely to pass along their genes.

A Fight Against Evolution?

Obesity is less a breakdown of willpower against temptation than it is a defeat in a struggle against the human genome itself, research suggests.

"We're on the threshold of a deep understanding of how obesity works," molecular biologist Jeffrey Friedman, of Rockefeller University and the Howard Hughes Medical Institute, told United Press International.

"In the meantime, we have to recognize how this battle against biology can make it intrinsically difficult to lose weight and not be judgmental of people who are not successful," Friedman added.

www.applesforhealth.com, February 14, 2003.

The new appetite for meat didn't mean we lost our passion for sweets, though. As Berkeley's Milton points out, the brain's growth may have been facilitated by abundant animal protein, but the brain operates on glucose, the sugar that serves as the major fuel for cellular function. "The brain drinks glucose 24 hours a day," she says. The sugars in fruit and the carbohydrates in edible grains and tubers are particularly good sources of glucose.

The appetite for meat and sweets was essential to human survival, but it didn't lead to obesity for several reasons. For one thing, the wild game our ancestors ate was high in protein but very low in fat—only about 4%, compared with up to 36% in grain-fed supermarket beef. For another, our ancestors couldn't count on a steady supply of any particular food. Hunters might bring down a deer or a rabbit, or nothing at all. Fruit might be in season, or it might not. A chunk of honeycomb might have as many calories as half a dozen Krispy Kreme doughnuts, but you might be able to get it once a year at best—and it wouldn't have the fat.

Beyond that, hunting and gathering took enormous physical work. Chasing wild animals with spears and clubs was a marathon undertaking—and then you had to hack up the catch and lug it miles back to camp. Climbing trees to find nuts and fruit was hard work, too. In essence, early humans ate what amounted to the best of the high-protein Atkins diet and the low-fat Ornish diet, and worked out almost nonstop. To get a sense of their endurance, cardiovascular fitness, musculature and body fat, say evolutionary anthropologists, look at a modern marathon runner.

That was the condition of pretty much the entire human race when anatomically modern humans first arose, between 150,000 and 100,000 years ago, and things stayed that way until what some anthropologists have called humanity's worst mistake: the invention of agriculture. We now had a steady source of food, but there were downsides as well. For one thing, our ancestors began gathering in much larger population centers, where bacteria and viruses could fester. Small bands of hunter-gatherers can spread disease only so far, but the birth of cities made epidemics possible for the first time.

Nutritionally, the shift away from wild meat, fruits and vegetables to a diet mostly of cultivated grain robbed humans of many of the essential amino acids, vitamins and minerals they had thrived on. Average life span increased, thanks to the greater abundance of food, but average height diminished. Skeletons also began to show an increase in calcium deficiency, anemia, bad teeth and bacterial infections. Most meat that people ate came from domesticated animals, which have more fat than wild game. Livestock also supplied early pastoralists with milk products, which are full of artery-clogging butterfat. But obesity still wasn't a problem, because even with animals to help, physical exertion was built into just about everyone's life.

That remained the case practically up to the present. It's really only in the past 100 years that cars and other machinery have dramatically reduced the need for physical labor. And as exercise has vanished from everyday life, the technology of food production has become much more sophisticated. In the year 1700 Britain consumed 23,000 tons of sugar. That was about 3.4 kg of sugar per capita. The U.S. currently consumes more than 68.2 kg of sweetener per capita, nearly 50% of which is high-fructose corn syrup that is increasingly used as a sugar substitute. Farmers armed with powerful fertilizers and high-tech equipment are growing enormous quantities of corn and wheat, most of which are processed and refined to be tastier and more convenient, but is less nutritious. They are raising vast herds of cattle whose meat is laden with the fat that makes it taste so good. They are producing milk, butter and cheese by the tankerload, again full of the fat that humans crave.

And thanks to mass production, all that food is relatively cheap. It's also absurdly convenient. In many areas of the U.S., if you had a craving for cookies a century ago, you had to fire up the woodstove and make the dough from scratch. If you wanted butter, you had to churn it. If you wanted a steak, you had to butcher the cow. Now you jump into the car and head for the nearest convenience store—or if that's too much effort, you pick up a phone or log on to the Internet and have the stuff delivered to your door.

Unless you make a determined effort, you'll probably choose the path of least resistance. Evolving during a time of scarcity, humans developed an instinctive desire for basic tastes—sweet, fat, salt—that they could never fully satisfy. As a result, says Rutgers University anthropologist Lionel Tiger, "we don't have a cut-off mechanism for eating. Our bodies tell us, 'Fat is good to eat but hard to get.'" The second half of that equation is no longer true, but the first remains a powerful drive.

This doesn't necessarily mean we're doomed. There's no doubt that the obesity epidemic is real and the West's collective health has been getting progressively worse. Indeed, says Yale public-health expert Dr. David Katz, "today's kids may be the first generation in history whose life expectancy is projected to be less than that of their parents."

But there's plenty of reason to hope that we'll get obesity under control. Researchers are hard at work trying to understand the basic biochemistry of hunger and fat metabolism; policymakers are pushing for better labels and nutritional information; school boards are giving their cafeteria menus a closer look and reconsidering vending-machine contracts with makers of sugary soft drinks; in the U.S., urban planners are rethinking cities and towns to get people out of the car and onto their feet; people are putting themselves on low-carb and low-calorie diets; and more and more foodmakers are beginning to see increased awareness of the obesity epidemic not as a threat but as a business opportunity.

It's too soon to tell if it's working, but there's at least one hopeful sign. For the first three quarters of 2003, there was no increase in obesity among adult Americans, according to preliminary data from the National Health Interview Survey.

Campaigns against smoking and drunk driving have raised the world's consciousness about these public-health issues dramatically. There's no reason to think an anti-obesity campaign can't do so as well—as long as everyone involved acknowledges that the problem is real and that solving it will be as hard as anything they've ever done. After all, it's not easy to fight millions of years of evolution.

Periodical Bibliography

The following articles have been selected to supplement the diverse views presented in this chapter.

American Legion Magazine	"The Waistline War," November 2003.
John Balzar	"Feast (Slowly) on the Buffet of Life," *Los Angeles Times*, December 23, 2001.
Doug Bandow	"It Ain't My Fault," *Chronicles*, September 2003.
Vicki Berkus	"America's Food Compulsion: Food Addiction," *Counselor*, June 2003.
Todd G. Buchholz	"Are Fast-Food Establishments Making Americans Fat?" *Journal of Controversial Medical Claims*, November 2003.
Arthur Frank and Glenn A. Gaesser	"Is Obesity a Disease?" *Family Practice News*, August 15, 2003.
Dave Fusaro	"Responsibility . . . on Both Sides," *Food Processing*, April 2004.
Erica Goode	"The Gorge-Yourself Environment," *New York Times*, July 22, 2003.
Alice Lesch Kelly	"Can We Downsize?" *Los Angeles Times*, April 5, 2004.
David S. Ludwig and Stephen L. Gortmaker	"Programming Obesity in Childhood," *Lancet*, July 17, 2004.
Ralph Nader	"McDonald's Seducing Children to a Deadly Diet," *Liberal Opinion Week*, March 18, 2002.
Clarence Page	"Here's a Good Exercise: Eat Less," *Liberal Opinion Week*, September 2, 2002.
Jacob Sullum	"The Anti-Pleasure Principle," *Reason*, July 2003.
James E. Tillotson	"Who's Filling Your Grocery Bag?" *Nutrition Today*, September/October 2004.
Jayachangran N. Variyam	"Technological Changes Contribute to Rise in Obesity," *Frozen Food Digest*, July 2004.

CHAPTER 3

What Is the Most Effective Way to Reduce Obesity?

Chapter Preface

In the late 1990s there was a new addition to the plethora of diets available to people trying to lose weight. Books such as *Dr. Atkins' New Diet Revolution*, *The South Beach Diet*, and *Enter the Zone* advocate different variations on low-carbohydrate, or "low-carb" diets. These diets are based on the belief that obesity is caused by carbohydrates rather than overeating, and they aim to help people lose weight by significantly reducing the carbohydrates they consume (but not their overall calorie intake). For people struggling with their weight, yet unable or unwilling to reduce their calorie intake, these diets often seem like the perfect solution for weight loss. However, critics allege that low-carb diets are ineffective and unhealthy. As a result, like many other diets, low-carb diets have become the subject of great debate.

There are hundreds of enthusiastic advocates of low-carb diets who claim that these diets have enabled them not only to lose weight but to keep it off permanently. For example, Zach Smith lost 183 pounds on the Zone diet and claims that it helps him maintain his new weight. He asserts, "I like to eat this way. It doesn't feel like any kind of restrictive means of eating. I find that it's real easy and I can see myself eating this way forever." James Wintershied, who is on the Atkins Diet, echoes Smith's experience. He explains, "After nine months on the program, I had shed 122 pounds and weighed 213, a weight I maintain. . . . Just the other night we went out for ice cream to celebrate [my son] Ethan's fifth birthday. No, I didn't indulge, and I didn't feel deprived. I felt alive!"

However, critics allege that low-carb diets are unhealthy and do not work over a long period of time. Low-carb followers often eat liberal amounts of meats and dairy products rather than carbohydrates like bread, fruit, and vegetables. Many nutrition experts and physicians believe this type of diet contributes to heart disease, diabetes, stroke, and other chronic health problems. Martha Weintraub, a nutrition specialist in the cardiology department at the University of Michigan Health System says, "People want magic—easy, fast results. . . . These diets are popular because they give fast results and are simple." However, she warns, "Many know it doesn't feel healthy and may have side effects." Researcher Patrick Johnson argues that in addition to possible health problems, there is no evidence for the long-term effectiveness of low-carb diets. "The idea that a single nutrient is to blame for the [obesity] problem has proven erroneous," he says. "It turned out not to be true with fat, and it appears to be erroneous with carbohydrates as well." Johnson concludes that, "At its simplest, weight loss still appears to involve the difficult task of increasing daily energy expenditure and lowering food intake."

For large numbers of obese people who struggle constantly, and unsuccessfully, to lose weight, the question of, "What is the most effective way to reduce obesity?" is of great importance. The following chapter offers various opinions on this contentious issue.

"[Gastric bypass surgery] has changed my life and given me back years that I lost being obese."

Gastric Bypass Surgery Is an Effective Way to Lose Weight

Nancy Naomi

Obese people suffer greatly—both physiologically and psychologically—explains Nancy Naomi in the following viewpoint. While gastric bypass surgery is a difficult experience, she grants, its benefits greatly outweigh that discomfort, she believes. Naomi argues that when other weight-loss efforts have not been successful, gastric bypass can help an obese person lose weight and regain a healthy, happy life. Naomi is a freelance writer living in Montreal, Quebec, Canada.

As you read, consider the following questions:

1. How many pounds did Naomi lose through gastric bypass surgery?
2. Why was the author surprised that no psychological testing was performed on her prior to surgery?
3. Why, as explained by Naomi, is it impossible for her to eat rib steak and pasta?

Nancy Naomi, "A Life-Altering Experience," *Diabetes Forecast*, vol. 56, April 2003, p. 128. Copyright © 2003 by the American Diabetes Association. Reproduced by permission from the American Diabetes Association.

M orbidly obese are the two most hideous words one can be called, yet 15 years ago [in 1988] that is all anyone in the medical profession seemed to call me. At 30, I was an insulin-using type 2 diabetic, weighing in at 280 pounds, the heaviest I had ever been. And though I dieted and exercised, I could not lose enough to make a difference.

How could I know, when I gratefully signed up to undergo gastric bypass surgery, that I would be born again as the thin me emerged. The surgeon told me that the most I could hope to lose would be 60 to 80 pounds and that I would probably level off at 200 pounds. Today, I weigh 152 pounds, and at 5'6" tall, I wear a size 12. I constantly watch what I eat, am careful to avoid overeating, and exercise five days a week in the gym. I am in the best shape of my life, physiologically and psychologically.

A Life-Altering Experience

But this is also a cautionary tale. "Stomach stapling," the euphemism for this serious surgery, is life altering. While losing weight is gratifying, especially for an overweight person with diabetes, the eating habits required for this lifestyle change are severely restrictive. Anyone who is not mentally prepared for this new, radical way of life may face dire consequences. The psyche of a morbidly obese person is unlike that of a thin person, and most doctors performing this surgery don't understand the profound impact of food deprivation.

Perhaps I coped well because the only change that occurred for me involved the quantity of food I ate, not its quality. Yet, food, or the lack of it, became the focal point of my life for up to two years following my operation. Virtually no psychological testing was performed on me prior to surgery, and that baffles me, knowing now what I was in store for. I couldn't accept that after eating a tablespoon of oatmeal I would be full, and that if I ate two, I would be nauseated to the point of vomiting up the entire contents of my stomach. To this day, there are times I leave the table hungry but not physically able to consume more—part of my brain wants to continue eating, yet I know I cannot physically swallow one more bite.

I've been insulin-free now for 14 years, although I did recently start taking [the diabetes pill] Glucophage. I have al-

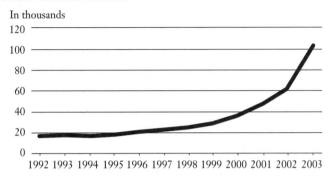

Estimated Number of Stomach Surgeries in the United States

In thousands

ways endeavored to keep tight control of my sugar levels, even at my highest weight. I consider myself fortunate for having never suffered from any ill effects as a result of my obesity.

I continue to thrive in excellent health and maintain strong bones due to weight training. I still can eat only three bites of a chicken breast with perhaps two teaspoons of mashed potato over a half-hour dinner period. Two pieces of sushi and I am bursting; one bite more will have me racing to the bathroom to vomit. Some foods are just out of the question because they are entirely too difficult to digest, such as rib steak and pasta.

But despite these drawbacks, I love the new me.

Would I get this surgery again? In a heartbeat. It has changed my life and given me back years that I lost being obese. I recommend it to anyone who, like me, has tried to lose weight carefully and consciously, but in vain.

"In the case of obesity, surgery is invoked to deal with a genuine health problem that could be dealt with in another way."

The Obese Should Not Undergo Gastric Bypass Surgery

Religion & Society Report

In the following viewpoint the *Religion & Society Report* argues that obesity is the result of a lack of self-control. The editors contend that the obese should not choose the easy solution of gastric bypass surgery. This surgery is a drastic and barbaric solution for a problem that should be dealt with by dieting, maintains the *Report*. The *Religion & Society Report* is a monthly periodical offering analysis of cultural controversies and public issues.

As you read, consider the following questions:
1. According to the *Religion & Society Report*, what questions does gastric bypass surgery raise?
2. Why is gastric surgery for young people truly barbaric, according to the *Report*?
3. Why is gastric bypass surgery "a kind of medical violence," according to the *Religion & Society Report*?

Religion & Society Report, "Medical Necessities," vol. 20, October, 2003, pp. 4–5. Copyright © 2003 by the Howard Center. Reproduced by permission.

In August [2003], the *Grand Rapids Press* announced a surprising medical development: "Blodgett [Hospital] opens up to gastric bypasses. The blooming weight-loss operation—there is a 600-case backlog—moved in following the exit of the birthing unit in early July." The hospital management seemed quite content with the loss of its obstetric facility and the substitution of a "bariatric" unit. "By October, we expect to be doing 40 cases per week," said John Mosely, the corporate vice president for development and strategic planning. This operation has been so well developed that in many cases it can be done laprascopically, without a major incision into the abdomen of the patient. It essentially shuts off a major part of the stomach from access to the food chain, reducing the capacity of the stomach available for any meal, and thus necessarily reducing the amount that can be eaten. It is an effective, dramatic, and one might almost say barbaric way of forcing seriously obese people to lose tens, perhaps hundreds of excess pounds.

Lack of Self-Control

Because obesity, often gross obesity, is rapidly becoming a nationwide problem, and because gross obesity represents a serious health risk as well as a professional and social handicap, this operation is gaining popularity with the terribly fat. Because it is virtually always elective surgery, it may not be covered by insurance and then must be paid for out of personal funds, relieving the surgeons and the hospitals of the necessity of wrangling with the insurance companies. Grand Rapids is a medium-sized city in Michigan: its population includes a substantial number with a Dutch and Calvinistic heritage, and one would normally expect self-control, rather than elective surgery, from those solid Midwesterners.

In a saner and less self-indulgent society, this drastic operation, which under some circumstances can be surgically reversed, would probably be considered only for the most extreme and stubborn cases, if then. Inasmuch as almost invariably the cause of the obesity is excessive eating, it ought to be possible to resolve the problem by dieting. Certainly a term in a concentration camp (which we are not recommending) would eliminate the obesity. Surgery seems to be

Lucky to Be Alive

While pregnant with daughter Tawnya, now [in 2003] 10, [Laura Lee] Turner put on 64 lbs. With her son Bruce Jr., 8, she gained 72. At 243 lbs., says the Moyock, N.C., home-maker, "my back hurt, my knees hurt, I had no energy." After friends told her about their gastric-bypass surgeries, Turner, 37, sought the help of Dr. Robert Brewer in Virginia Beach, Va. Wanting to be thin and "able to do more with my kids," she underwent the operation in December '96.

In just a year the 5'8" Turner dropped to a rail-thin 98 lbs. "I was very tiny, looked hollow, and my hair came out in patches," says Turner, who by then needed a feeding tube to stay alive. A new doctor found bleeding ulcers and a hole where her stomach was stapled; two corrective surgeries also failed. While Turner was out with Tawnya in the fall of 1998, her feeding tube broke, she says, spilling the contents of her stomach onto her.

Her marriage suffered, and in September 2001 she and her husband, Bruce, divorced. She now lives with auto mechanic John Winall, 28, who saw her through a successful fourth surgery last July. Turner, who today weighs 126 lbs., won a $550,000 settlement from the hospital where her second and third surgeries took place. With skin hanging around her mid-dle due to the weight loss, she says, "I need a tummy tuck." But a fifth surgery isn't likely, she adds: "I'm scared of scalpels."

People Weekly, March 10, 2003.

---

an easy way out, but to resort to it raises questions about the moral strength of the patients and the judgment of the physicians. Gastric bypass surgery is now proposed and exe-cuted for young people, even for teenagers and preteens. The thought of sending an otherwise properly formed young person off for the rest of his or her life with a muti-lated digestive system is truly barbaric.

The Desire to Act Without Consequences

According to G. Steven Suits, M.D., gastric bypass surgery is only one example of the modern desire to be able to live and act exactly as one chooses without medical or other conse-quences (apart, of course, from a costly operation). Other ex-amples abound, from the simple desire to be able to age with-out showing it to the sad drive to change one's sex, or to be able to act as though it were changed. In every large population center in the United States, one will be confronted with advertisements in print and on the air for cosmetic surgery of all kinds. These procedures sometimes take on rather bizarre forms, from botox injections to remove wrinkles by paralyzing small facial muscles through breast reduction or enlargement to lioposuction to remove unwanted fat. Gastric bypass surgery is only the most dramatic of the various procedures that are available.

Medical ethicists regularly debate end of life issues. So far little attention has been devoted to elective operations. Operations that the rational mind would consider not merely elective but mutilating, such as "sex change" procedures, are increasingly accepted, often paid for by insurance, and compared to them, perhaps gastric bypass surgery is relatively innocuous.

From the Sabre to the Scalpel

In earlier societies, even in nineteenth-century America, individuals who felt themselves insulted sometimes settled things by a duel with swords or pistols. This is how our first Secretary of the Treasury, Alexander Hamilton, met his end. Today we feel that insults to one's pride or vanity should be dealt with less violently. In place of swords and pistols, we have introduced a kind of medical violence to deal not with insults, but with other damages to vanity such as being too fat or too wrinkled. In the case of obesity, surgery is invoked to deal with a genuine health problem that could be dealt with in another way. It is interesting that Blodgett Hospital in Grand Rapids has replaced its birthing facilities with bariatric ones. Grand Rapids has other places for pregnant women to deliver their babies, but is there not something symbolic—and sad—about abandoning care for pregnant mothers and newborn babies to serve those suffering from gross obesity through lack of discipline and self-control?

"*We have good reasons to hope for the development of safe and effective [drugs] . . . to assist people in achieving and maintaining healthy weight.*"

Weight-Loss Drugs Should Be Developed to Help Reduce Obesity

Lester M. Crawford

In the following viewpoint Lester M. Crawford argues that while obesity needs to be addressed on multiple fronts, one of the most effective solutions is weight-loss drugs. Crawford explains that although safe and effective weight-loss drugs are not currently available, they can be developed. He advocates increased research to facilitate the development of these critical tools to fight obesity. Crawford is acting commissioner of the U.S. Food and Drug Administration, the federal agency responsible for ensuring the safety of the nation's food and drugs.

As you read, consider the following questions:

1. As stated by Crawford, how much does obesity cost the United States every year?
2. What did the Obesity Working Group conclude about the cause of obesity, as explained by the author?
3. How effective are currently available drug therapies for obesity, according to Crawford?

Lester M. Crawford, keynote address at the World Obesity Congress & Expo, July 12, 2004.

I am delighted to participate in this conference called to examine potential answers to a major public health concern affecting practically the entire world. It's a concern that's high on the health care agenda of countries on every continent—an issue of growing seriousness and prominence not only among industrialized nations, but also in some parts of the Third World. In the United States, this issue commands the closest attention of the Department of Health and Human Services and, in particular, of the agency I have the honor to represent, the Food and Drug Administration [FDA].

I am talking, of course, about the epidemic of overweight and obesity, an unforeseen and unwelcome adverse effect of the proud achievement of our food producers and modern technology, which is the overflowing horn of plenty.

A Runaway Problem

At the FDA, we are accountable for the safety and the wholesome nature of 80 percent of our national food supply —practically everything we eat except for beef, poultry, and a few egg products. This responsibility, in addition to our general duty to protect and promote the public health, has placed our agency in the forefront of our government's efforts to bring the runaway excess-weight problem under control.

And a major problem it is: overweight and obesity affect about two out of every three Americans—and, what is even more alarming, 15 percent of our children and adolescents. These extra pounds are ruinous to health by increasing the risks for a host of diseases that are inflating our nation's morbidity and mortality statistics. According to the most recent estimates, obesity is a causative factor in as many as 400,000 deaths each year, which makes it the second most devastating avoidable cause of premature death in the United States after tobacco.

Moreover, while smoking is on the decline, overweight and obesity statistics are relentlessly rising, and threaten to erode the substantial gains in life expectancy and quality of life that have been won by modern medicine. While the resulting human suffering is the most dire aspect of this epidemic, its economic consequences accentuate the hardship.

The costs of obesity-associated health care and lost productivity are currently estimated at $117 billion a year.

The Obesity Working Group

For us at the FDA, this ominous drift into disease and expense presents a tremendous challenge that—although not at our doorsteps alone—we know we must confront with all available powers and resources. Last August [2003], we therefore appointed an expert Obesity Working Group and charged it with two basic tasks: exploring the critical dimensions of the excess-weight problem, and devising a plan how to address it.

The group's probe was a major undertaking. Our working group consisted of 17 FDA senior scientists and staffers who were backed by more than 40 specialists researching the various issues under study. We were briefed by experts from other government agencies; consulted with the public and academia; met with representatives of the packaged food and restaurant industries; and solicited and reviewed scores of expert comments on various aspects of the obesity epidemic.

Effective Drugs "Just Around the Corner"

For years we've been hearing that more effective weight-loss drugs are just around the corner. But in the past 27 years, only two anti-obesity drugs have been approved, and those drugs have a modest weight loss profile. . . .

But now, better weight loss drugs really are just around the corner, with the first approvals just a few short years away.

Obesity Meds and Research News, June 6, 2001. www.obesity-news.com.

We dug deep into scientific literature—to give you one example, our report, which was released in March [2004], includes 50 references to studies and professional articles dealing with nutrition labeling of packaged goods and in restaurants, which is just one of the eight key issues we examined. In addition to surveying what's known, we also identified knowledge gaps that need to be filled, and recommended areas for further biomedical and social sciences research.

We explored the effectiveness of obesity-related messages in the public and private sectors, and examined various education programs for promoting healthy nutrition. And we surveyed existing therapies for mitigating obesity.

What have we learned? The overriding lesson of our inquiry is that the epidemic has no single cause: rather, it is the confluence of numerous factors acting together over time. Ergo, our second key conclusion is that the epidemic will have no simple or speedy solution. Controlling obesity will be a long-term process requiring coordinated and comprehensive efforts on many fronts. . . .

Short-Term Measures Do Not Work

The concept of extreme body weight as illness is hardly new: already in the 5th century B.C., Hippocrates noted that "sudden death is more common in those who are naturally fat than in the lean," and in 1760, a Scottish physician named Flemyng wrote that "corpulency, when in an extraordinary degree, may be reckoned as a disease, as it in some measure obstructs the free exercise of the animal functions; and hath a tendency to shorten life, by paving the way to dangerous distempers."

But while many of these "distempers"—which we now know range from cardiovascular hypertension and congestive heart failure to diabetes, stroke, osteoarthritis, and psychological disorders—have been frequently and successfully addressed by pharmaceutical R&D [research and development], attempts to develop a remedy for the underlying condition have repeatedly failed to demonstrate adequate effectiveness and safety.

One of the earliest obesity therapeutics, first used in the 1880s, was thyroid extract. It induced weight loss by causing hyperthyroidism, itself adverse to health. Dinitrophenol, introduced in the 1930s, is a highly dangerous agent that causes cataracts and neuropathy and, even worse, all too often results in hyperthermia, metabolic collapse, and death. Amphetamines and their congeners, prescribed since the late 1930's, dominate the field of weight-control medicine, but have the down side of being potentially addictive, subject to abuse, and are not ideal in a population at risk for heart disease.

Over time, and particularly in recent years, the medical community has come to recognize that short-term measures to address obesity don't adequately reduce the long-term risks associated with excess weight. As we all now know and understand, obesity is a chronic condition associated with wide-ranging derangements of energy metabolism. Over the long term, that increases the risk for numerous serious and life-threatening diseases.

Effective Drugs Are Needed

Based on this understanding, and following the recommendations of an advisory committee, our agency in 1996 issued a draft guidance that set the framework for the development of chronic-use drugs to treat obesity. The document called for long-term clinical trials of safety and efficacy, and set forth standards of effectiveness in the hope of fostering the development of a crop of chronic-use preventives and remedies that would ultimately reduce the disease risks of obesity.

Since then, our agency has approved three long-term treatments for weight control: dexfenfluramine, sibutramine and orlistat. Dexfenfluramine, which took the market by storm in a popular combination regimen with phentermine, was withdrawn within 18 months of approval after it was shown to be associated with valvulopathy [heart disease]. This was an effect not predicted by any of the premarket data, whether in animals or in patients. Sibutramine is an effective drug, but it causes increases in pulse and blood pressure in some individuals, and requires careful monitoring. Orlistat, like sibutramine, is modestly effective, though apparently very safe.

In sum, a highly effective drug-based treatment for overweight and obesity is, today, sorely lacking in the medical armamentarium. Available therapies are only modestly effective, by no means so in all treated patients, and have no lasting effect once the use of the drug is stopped, thus necessitating life-long therapy in many individuals. We have no cure for obesity. Furthermore, there has never been a therapeutic class whose progress has been more vehemently buffeted by opposing desires for a true cure and concerns about drug risk—concerns that are frequently accompanied by arguments that obesity should be addressed with behavior modification. Obesity therapeutics is an exceedingly difficult area in which to work.

An Urgent Need

At the same time, one of the most encouraging conclusions of our working group is that opportunities for safer and more effective obesity drugs abound, and that the future of weight-control therapies is potentially bright. The list of molecular targets and mechanistic approaches is long, and grows daily thanks to vigorous basic research in this field. We have good reasons to hope for the development of safe and effective single-drug therapies and combination regimens to assist people in achieving and maintaining healthy weight. . . .

The millions of Americans—and people worldwide—with excess weight problem urgently need the same type of option that exists for a myriad of other health conditions and ailments. We must join efforts to overcome the hurdles and gaps of knowledge that stand in the way, and provide them with safe and effective therapies.

"There is no panacea for weight loss. There's no magic pill."

Weight-Loss Drugs Are Not the Best Way to Reduce Obesity

Robert C. Atkins

In the following viewpoint Robert C. Atkins asserts that weight-loss drugs are not an effective solution for obesity. While pharmaceutical companies offer many such drugs, they are either ineffective or unsafe, maintains Atkins. He believes that maintaining a healthy diet and exercising is the only effective way to achieve and maintain a healthy weight. Atkins is the creator of the Atkins Diet—a popular high-protein, high-fat, low carbohydrate diet—and author of *Dr. Atkins' New Diet Revolution.*

As you read, consider the following questions:

1. Why was fen-phen pulled from the market in 1997, according to Atkins?
2. How does the effectiveness of sibutramine compare to the effectiveness of diet and exercise alone, as explained by the author?
3. Why does Atkins believe that all appetite suppressors are really appetite postponers?

In Greek legend, Panacea was one of the daughters of Asclepius, the god of medicine and healing. She came to personify the power of healing through herbs, and her name, meaning "heal-all" or "universal cure," was applied to a mythical herb that could heal anything. It's from this minor Greek goddess that we get our modern word "panacea," meaning a nonexistent medicine that remedies all afflictions.

That's the myth. Now here's the reality: There *is* no panacea for weight loss. There's no magic pill—there isn't even a magic diet. The only true way to safe, permanent weight loss is through a lifestyle that combines a healthy diet with physical activity. But that doesn't keep the pharmaceutical industry from trying to convince us otherwise.

Ineffective and Unsafe Drugs

In my many years as a physician, I've seen all sorts of so-called miracle drugs for weight loss come and go. Some were ineffective but basically harmless, but others turned out to be downright dangerous. In the 1950s and '60s amphetamines were often prescribed for weight loss, with predictably disastrous consequences for the patients. In the late 1990s, deaths and serious health problems resulting from the use of fen-phen were grabbing the headlines. This treatment involved a combination of drugs: dexfenfluramine, sold under the brand name Redux®, or fenfluramine, sold under the brand name Pondimin®, and phentermine. Even though fenfluramine had already been linked to a very serious side effect called primary pulmonary hypertension, the combination was approved by the FDA [Food and Drug Administration] in 1996—the first new diet drug to receive such approval in 20 years.

The fen-phen combination was wildly popular. In the first year after approval, 18 million prescriptions for the drug combination were filled. In the second year, however, numerous cases of heart valve damage and pulmonary hypertension began to show up among people who used the drugs. In October 1997, the FDA pulled fen-phen from the market.

A Dangerous Choice for Weight Loss

Another prescription weight-loss drug is sibutramine (Meridia®). This medication reduces your appetite by affecting the

Looking for a Quick Fix

It's the irony of our times, everyone wants something for nothing—that is weight loss with no effort—the quick fix—the magic cure! And we want it now! Unfortunately, there is usually a price to pay and it usually affects our health.

A former colleague stopped in the other day to share her recent experience on [the weight-loss drug] fen-phen. Like the majority of the people using these drugs, she had only a vague idea how they work. She believed they would raise her metabolism and help her burn fat. (They have no effect on metabolism and do not burn fat.) My friend didn't have time to "diet," felt desperate and turned to a quick fix. Seven hundred dollars and three months later she had only lost ten pounds. Then the clinic staff informed her she would have to take a "drug holiday" because FDA [Federal Drug Administration] guidelines state they should only be used consecutively for 90 days.

The rebound of coming off them left her so low she could barely drag herself out of bed the next week. She begged the doctor to allow her to start them again, and so a week later she was back on her prescription for another 90 days. . . .

So why do so many people play Russian roulette with these diet drugs? Because, like my colleague, they are desperate. The dietary laws of the past ten years are not working for them and the lure of the quick fix tempts them to try drugs that may prove unhealthy in the long run. If they could slow down long enough to really listen to their inner voice and to their body, they would not subject themselves to these drugs in the first place.

Nutritional Weight and Wellness, 2004. www.weightandwellness.com.

serotonin level in your brain, just as drugs such as fluoxetine (Prozac®) and sertraline (Zoloft®) do. It helps only about six out of 10 people who take it, and it doesn't even help them very much. When this drug is combined with a reduced-calorie diet and an exercise program, patients lose on average a grand total of about four pounds in the first four weeks. In other words, they lose about as much weight taking the drug as they're likely to lose with diet and exercise alone—but are faced with the additional risk of having the medication elevate their blood pressure.

Perhaps the most widely prescribed weight-loss drug today is orlistat (Xenical®). This drug works by blocking the absorption of about a third of the fat you eat. It has a number of unpleasant and even dangerous side effects, it's very expensive and for most patients it doesn't work very well. Most people lose some weight during the first six months, and then stall well above their goal weight. The weight goes right back on as soon as they stop taking the drug. In fact, all appetite suppressers are in reality appetite postponers. When the majority of people who have taken diet pills stop, they gain more weight than they had lost.

Ephedra is now front of mind because of the tragic death of Baltimore Orioles pitcher Steve Bechler. [Update: Bechler died in February 2003. In December of that year, the Federal government banned the sale of ephedra, but in April 2005, a Federal judge in Utah struck down the ruling, which opens the door for other states to do the same.] However, unlike the panaceas mentioned above, ephedra is not a prescription drug but a herb. It comes in a variety of convenient forms, from pills to chocolate bars to soft drinks. A widely used weight-loss panacea, the promoters of this stimulant claim that it has near-magical thermogenic (fat-burning) powers. Aside from not working very well for weight loss, it can cause a stroke when taken beyond recommended doses.

Where does the long, sorry history of weight-loss panaceas leave us? Right back where we should have been all along: losing weight and keeping it off by combining a controlled carbohydrate intake with a regimen of regular exercise. Controlling appetite, which is key to losing weight, requires stabilization of blood sugar. This can be achieved by eating regular meals and snacks that include protein and natural fats and avoiding added sugars, bleached white flour, and other highly refined carbohydrates.

In contrast, diet pills work only as long as you take them. What happens if they produce side effects you can't tolerate are aren't willing to risk? What if you must discontinue them because you can no longer afford them? What happens if they are taken off the market? Diet pills are a poor short-term solution to a long-term problem.

| "*Legal action could be a powerful weapon against the public health problem of obesity.*"

Lawsuits Against Fast Food Restaurants Are an Effective Way to Combat Obesity

John H. Banzhaf III

The following viewpoint is excerpted from congressional testimony given in 2003 by John H. Banzhaf III. Banzhaf opposes the Personal Responsibility in Food Consumption Act—subsequently passed in March 2004—which limits lawsuits against the fast food industry for obesity or weight gain–related problems. Banzhaf argues that the ability to file these lawsuits is a powerful way to keep the fast food industry accountable for the food it sells, and to force it to take actions to help counter the obesity epidemic. Banzhaf is a professor at George Washington University Law School in Washington, D.C.

As you read, consider the following questions:
1. How are consumers being fooled by restaurants, as argued by the author?
2. How does Banzhaf reply to charges by the food industry that lawsuits against them are frivolous?
3. According to the author, what do lawsuits against the tobacco industry teach about lawsuits against the food industry?

John H. Banzhaf III, testimony before the U.S. House Subcommittee on Commercial and Administrative Law, Committee on the Judiciary, Washington, DC, June 19, 2003.

In 2001 the U.S. Surgeon General issued a report showing that the U.S. was suffering from an epidemic of obesity which annually killed about 300,000 Americans and cost us over $100 billion a year. Since that time Congress has done virtually nothing of consequence to deal with this problem, just as for many years it did nothing of consequence to address the problem of smoking.

However, since I first proposed that legal action could be a powerful weapon against the public health problem of obesity, just as I had suggested—and then helped prove—that it could be a powerful weapon against the problem of smoking, the mere threat of legal action has proven to be very effective. For example, numerous articles and reports have noted that the threats of law suits have already prompted many food companies to take steps likely to reduce obesity.

The Personal Responsibility in Food Consumption Act

Yet some Members, not content to simply shirk Congress' responsibility to do something meaningful and effective about America's second most important and expensive preventable health problem, now support an industry-sponsored bailout and protection bill[1] to end what seems to be one of the few effective tools against this problem. FOR SHAME! If it ain't broke, don't fix it, especially until Congress is prepared to adopt comprehensive legislation to help save taxpayers more than $50 BILLION annually in obesity costs.

This bill is based upon two faulty assumptions. The FIRST is that the problem is caused by a lack of personal responsibility. But virtually everyone agrees that this epidemic rise in obesity and in obesity-related diseases occurred largely within the past 15–20 years, and there is no evidence that there has been a corresponding drop in personal and/or parental responsibility.

The SECOND faulty assumption is that, contrary to virtually every serious study, the fast food industry—with its misleading advertising, failure to clearly and conspicuously disclose nutritional information (as all other foods do) and/or

1. The bill passed in March 2004.

to provide any warnings of the type common to many other products which present risks which are less serious but even better known—is such an insignificant cause of obesity in all cases (including those regarding children) that it deserves unprecedented absolute immunity from all liability.

Consumers Are Being Fooled

As the business-oriented *Wall Street Journal* recently noted in "That Veggie Wrap You Just Chowed Down Is More Fattening Than a Ham Sandwich" [1/14/03]: "HERE'S A FAST-FOOD nutrition quiz. Which has the fewest calories: a McDonald's Quarter Pounder with Cheese, Panera's Smoked Ham and Swiss sandwich, or Baja Fresh's grilled chicken salad? Surprisingly, it's a Quarter Pounder. The answer is likely to shock diners who are flocking to trendy new eateries such as Fresh City, Baja Fresh Mexican Grill and Panera Bread, all of which promise fresh, nonfried and healthy-sounding fare . . . the truth is that these and other wraps, salads and sandwiches being hyped as a healthy alternative to fast food are loaded with calories and fat. . . . While the restaurant chains don't make any specific claims about the healthfulness or calorie content of their menu items, they nonetheless give consumers the impression that they are offering healthier food. . . . But consumers are being fooled. . . . But making the healthy choice can be tough. Most restaurants don't display nutrition information inside the restaurant, and the menu offerings often are deceptive. . . . Nutritionists argue that calorie information should be available at the ordering counter."

Warnings, after all, are not designed only for the best and brightest, but also for those with less education; less wisdom, judgment or maturity; and those who may be momentarily forgetful.

For those who then argue that food companies should escape all liability because children's obesity is caused solely by a lack of parental responsibility, the simple answer is that the law does not blame children for the lack of care of their parents, so long as the harm was reasonably foreseeable by the defendant. For example, when McDonald's gives out tiny action figures with its children's meals, it is very careful to warn in big letters of the choking danger present if the toys are given to infants—even though that danger is clearly common knowledge. McDonald's knows that, if a child choked on a part from the toy and suffered brain damage, McDonald's would be held liable for its fair share of the medical costs—despite the clear negligence of the parents—provided that it could have foreseen that this would happen.

With regard to meals served to children, and even meals like Happy Meals and Mighty Kids Meals intended solely for children, McDonald's provides no warnings whatsoever.

A Changing Menu at McDonald's

Many [fast food companies] are having to overhaul their product lines because of the growing concern of consumers and governments about obesity. . . .

McDonald's is now offering more healthy choices. Earlier this year [2004], it decided to phase out its "supersize" portions of fries and soft drinks. In America this month [May 2004] it launched an "Adult Happy Meal" that includes a salad, bottled water, a pedometer and a booklet of walking tips. Charlie Bell, McDonald's new boss, says this has helped to boost takings. Comparable sales for its 30,000 restaurants in April were 10.5% higher than a year earlier.

Economist, May 22, 2004.

Neither proposition can be seriously advanced, much less proven, and the public seemingly is rejecting them and is prepared to hold the industry liable in law suits.

The industry and its spokesmen claim that all such law suits are frivolous, but industries do not need protection against law suits which are truly frivolous, only those law suits which judges, juries, and appellate courts are likely to take seriously. In this regard note that the smoker law suits, the nonsmoker law suits, and the law suits by the states against the tobacco industry, all were initially called frivolous. But they have all proven their worth, and helped to make a significant dent in the public health problem of smoking.

The industry itself has paid for full-page ads in national magazines attacking the suits, and has written Op-Ed pieces opposing them. But their very concern and attention to these legal actions clearly belies any suggestion that the industry regards them as merely frivolous.

Looking Back at the Tobacco Law Suits

Even the lawyers who represented smokers in such suits were reluctant to represent *NON*smokers in suits against the tobacco industry, believing that such suits had little if any chance of success. But one husband-and-wife team has already won $300 million in the first round of a class action nonsmoker law suit, and individual nonsmoking plaintiffs are beginning to win also.

Finally, even anti-tobacco lawyers were so sure that state law suits against the industry could not possibly succeed that most refused to take them on, and the few that did were called "crazy." Today, of course, we call them multi-millionaires, since these law suits—likewise termed "frivolous" in their day —have now resulted in a settlement of over $240 BILLION dollars.

As one reporter, after talking to many legal experts of all sides of the issue put it: "All the legal experts I talked to agreed on one thing: After tobacco overturned years of legal precedent, you can't say any lawsuit is impossible."

Many articles and reports have suggested that more progress has been made regarding the problem of smoking than any other major public health problem: e.g., abuse of alcohol, illicit drug use, teenage pregnancies, etc. Clearly this is due in large part to the effective use of a wide variety of different kinds of legal actions—exactly what is being planned now with regard to obesity.

Premature Action

In this bill Congress assumes that it can pre-determine that in no set of facts involving food litigation should any company be held liable, even for its fair share of the resulting costs. This is presumptuous as well as preposterous, since the bill covers many situations in which most would agree that there should be liability. It also departs from the 200-year-old tradition of letting courts first decide new cases as they arise, and then stepping in to "correct" the process only if the results prove to be clearly contrary to the public interest.

This is especially egregious here because the bill unreasonably and unnecessarily interferes with the rights of states to have their courts decide these issues, at least initially, and is so broad that it seems to affect matters having no relationship to "interstate commerce" and therefore may be, as the U.S. Supreme Court has recently reminded us, beyond Congress' ability to legislate.

For all of these and other reasons, it is respectfully suggested that it is premature—if not presumptuous and preposterous—for Congress at this time to conclude that the one weapon against the war on obesity which appears to be having an impact should be eliminated; that it can decide without waiting for state court trial and appellate judges to consider the myriad of factual situations, legal arguments, and still-undiscovered evidence which may be presented in these trials that no such plaintiffs should even have their day in court; and that an industry should be given unprecedented immunity from all liability without any showing of harm or even serious danger.

Instead, Congress should consider comprehensive legislation aimed at America's epidemic of obesity, wait to see what the effect of the legislative remedies and of fat litigation may be, and then and only then even consider some form of limited immunity. . . .

The Power of Legislation

Both the author and those involved in the movement to use legal action as a weapon against obesity have frequently stated that legislation is far preferable to litigation. Legislation can accomplish more, be applied fairly across the board, and affect many practices that litigation cannot reach. Here are only a few proposals which Congress may wish to consider before it abdicates its own responsibility to regulate, and simply grants the industry unnecessary blanket immunity:

A. Require that all fast food restaurants display information about the calories and fat in their menu items at the point of purchase when patrons are considering their choices while standing in line, not buried on a web site or on a hard-to-find pamphlet or back wall. Several state bills to require this have been introduced, and Congressional action would avoid confusion due to lack of uniformity.

B. Require that all fast food restaurants provide appropriate warnings about the danger of eating fattening fast food too often. PepsiCo has promised to do this, and McDonald's is already doing it in France.

C. Require that all fast food restaurants provide more nutritious alternative menu choices for people who find it inconvenient to eat elsewhere and who want to avoid the many fattening foods which all too frequently are their only choices.

D. Require that all food items intended for young children—e.g., Mighty Kids Meals, Lunchables, etc.—provide information about fat and calorie content not only in terms of adult nutritional requirements but also in terms of the vastly lower requirements for young children so that parents can knowledgeably exercise the parental responsibility they are urged to.

Should the fast food restaurants do these things—either voluntarily or as a result of uniform legislation—it would appear that they would largely insulate themselves from potential liability. This is a far better approach than simply granting them unearned immunity.

*"The threat of . . . lawsuits can do no good
to the employees, shareholders, or customers
of fast food firms."*

Lawsuits Against Fast Food Restaurants Are Not an Effective Way to Combat Obesity

Todd G. Buchholz

Consumers, not the food industry, are responsible for obesity, argues Todd G. Buchholz in the following viewpoint. He believes that lawsuits alleging food industry harm to buyers are absurd. According to him, there is no evidence that fast food is causing obesity; instead, Buchholz maintains, obesity is a result of larger portions eaten at home and increased snacking. Buchholz, who served as an economic adviser in the George H.W. Bush administration, is the author of *Market Shock*.

As you read, consider the following questions:
1. What is the key similarity between the tobacco lawsuits and claims against the fast food industry, as argued by Buchholz?
2. According to the author, how does Body Mass Index data disprove the hypothesis that fast food is to blame for obesity?
3. What adverse effects will lawsuits against the fast food industry have, in the author's view?

A scene: The overweight baseball fan jumps to his feet in the bleachers of Wrigley Field, screaming for the Chicago Cubs to hold onto their 3-2 lead in the bottom of the ninth inning. He squeezes a Cubs pennant in his left hand while shoving a mustard-smeared hot dog into his mouth with the right. The Dodgers have a runner on first, who is sneaking a big lead off the base. The Cubs' pitcher has thrown three balls and two strikes to the batter, a notorious power hitter. The obese fan holds his breath while the pitcher winds up and fires a blazing fastball. "Crack!" The ball flies over the fan's head into the bleachers for a game-winning home run. The fan slumps to his bleacher seat and has a heart attack.

Whom should the fan sue? (a) The Cubs for breaking his heart? (b) The hot dog company for making a fatty food? (c) The hot dog vendor for selling him a fatty food? (d) All of the above

A few years ago these questions might have seemed preposterous. But now scenes better suited for the absurd stories of [author Franz] Kafka snake their way into serious courtroom encounters. While no federal court has yet heard a case on behalf of sulking baseball fans, last year [2003] the U.S. District Court for the Southern District of New York responded to a complaint filed against McDonald's by a class of obese customers, alleging among other things that the company acted negligently in selling foods that were high in cholesterol, fat, salt, and sugar. In the past 10 years we have seen an outburst of class action lawsuits that alleged harm to buyers. With classes numbering in the thousands, these suits may bring great riches to tort lawyers, even if they provide little relief to the plaintiffs. The sheer size of the claims and the number of claimants often intimidate defending firms, which fear that their reputations will be tarnished in the media and their stock prices will be punished—not because of the merits but from the ensuing publicity. In his opinion in the McDonald's case, Judge Robert W. Sweet suggested that the McDonald's suit could "spawn thousands of similar 'McLawsuits' against restaurants." Recent books with titles like *Fat Land* and *Fast Food Nation* promote the view that fast food firms are harming our health and turning us into a people who are forced to shop in the "big and tall" section of the clothing stores. The *Wall Street Journal* recently reported that "big and tall" has become a $6 billion business in menswear, "representing more than a 10 percent share of the total men's market."

134

But before the legal attack on fast food gets too far along, it would be useful to look at the facts behind fast food and fat America and to ask whether the courtroom is really the place to determine what and where people should eat.

Fast food restaurants have exploded in popularity since World War II. More cars, more suburbs, and more roads have made roadside eating more convenient. During the 1950s, drive-through and drive-in hamburger, ice cream, and pizza joints catered to a mobile population. McDonald's, which specialized in roadside restaurants, eclipsed White Castle hamburger stands in the 1960s because the latter had focused more on urban walk-up customers. The McDonald's road signs in the early 1960s boasted of serving 1 million hamburgers; now McDonald's claims to have sold over 99 billion. The "zeros" in 100 billion will not fit on the firm's tote-board signs when the one-hundred-billionth burger is sold.

And yet, despite the popularity of such firms as McDonald's, Wendy's, Burger King, Pizza Hut, Taco Bell, and Subway—at which American consumers voluntarily spend over $100 billion annually—it has become fashionable to denounce these restaurants for a variety of sins: "They make people fat." "They hypnotize the kids." "They bribe the kids with toys." "They destroy our taste for more sophisticated foods." These condemnations often come from highbrow observers who claim that fast food customers are too ignorant or too blinded to understand what they are putting in their own mouths. The onslaught of criticism is not limited to the food. Animal rights activists condemn fast food outlets for animal cruelty. Environmentalists allege that fast food produces too much "McLitter." Orthodox organic food fans accuse fast food firms of using genetically modified ingredients, which they call "frankenfoods." In Europe, antiglobalization protestors allege that fast food homogenizes culture and spreads capitalism far and wide.

With the fury directed at fast food firms, it is no surprise that tort lawyers have jumped into the fray. Tort lawyers around the country settled the $246 billion tobacco case in 1998.[1] Those who have not retired on their stake from that

1. Cigarette makers settled with forty-six states over health costs for treating sick smokers.

settlement are wondering whether fast food could be the "next tobacco," along with HMOs [health maintenance organizations] and lead paint. After all, the surgeon general estimates that obesity creates about $115 billion in annual health care costs. There are differences, of course. No one, so far, has shown that cheeseburgers are chemically addictive. Furthermore, most fast food restaurants freely distribute their nutritional content and offer a variety of meals, some high in fat, some not. Nor is it clear that the average fast food meal is significantly less nutritious than the average restaurant meal, or even the average home meal. The iconic 1943 [artist] Norman Rockwell Thanksgiving painting ("Freedom from Want") highlights a plump turkey, which is high in protein. But surely the proud hostess has also prepared gravy, stuffing, and a rich pie for dessert—which, though undoubtedly tasty, would not win a round of applause from nutritionists.

The key similarity between the tobacco lawsuits and claims against the fast food industry is this: Both industries have deep pockets and millions of customers who could join as potential plaintiffs. Therefore, lawyers have enormous incentives to squeeze food complaints into the nation's courtrooms. They will not disappoint in their eagerness to pursue this course.

Changing Diets, Misplaced Blame

If you believe the old saying "you are what you eat," human beings are not what they used to be. . . .

Just as life expectancy in the United States rose almost steadily from about 47 years in 1900 to 80 years today, so too has the "Body Mass Index," or BMI, a ratio of height to weight. In the late nineteenth century, most people died too soon and were, simply put, too skinny. The two are related, of course. For most of human history only the wealthy were plump; paintings of patrons by [artist] Peter Paul Rubens illustrated that relationship. In ancient times figurines of [Roman goddess] Venus (carved thousands of years ago) displayed chunky thighs, big bellies, and BMIs far above today's obesity levels. Likewise, skinny people looked suspicious to the ancients. (Remember that the backstabbing Cassius[2] had

2. a Roman commander who conspired against Julius Caesar

a "lean and hungry look.") The rise in the BMI from the nineteenth century to about 1960 should be counted as one of the great social and medical victories of modern times. In a sense, it created a more equal social status, as well as a more equal physical stature.

So what went wrong more recently? It is not the case that the average BMI has suddenly accelerated. In fact, the BMI has been rising fairly steadily for the past 120 years. Nonetheless, since the 1960s the higher BMI scores have surpassed the optimal zone of about 20 to 25. No doubt, a more sedentary lifestyle adds to this concern. (In contrast, the healthy rise in BMIs during the early 1900s might be attributed to gaining more muscle, which weighs more than fat.) The post-1960s rise in BMI scores is similar to a tree that grows 12 inches per year but in its tenth year starts casting an unwanted shadow on your patio. In the case of people, more mass from fat has diminishing returns, cutting down their life spans and raising the risk for diabetes, heart disease, gallbladder disease, and even cancer. Over half of American adults are overweight, and nearly a quarter actually qualify as obese, according to the National Institutes of Health.

What the Data Show

Should we chiefly blame fast food for BMIs over 25? According to the caricature described by lawyers suing fast food companies, poor, ill-educated people are duped by duplicitous restaurant franchises into biting into greasy hamburgers and french fries. The data, however, tell us that this theory is wrong. If the "blame fast food" hypothesis were correct, we would see a faster pace of BMI growth among poorly educated people, who might not be able to read or understand nutritional labels. In fact, college-educated people—not the poorly educated—accounted for the most rapid growth in BMI scores between the 1970s and the 1990s. (Poorly educated people still have a higher overall incidence of obesity.) The percentage of obese college-educated women nearly tripled between the early 1970s and the early 1990s. In comparison, the proportion of obese women without high school degrees rose by only 58 percent. Among men, the results were similar. Obesity among those without high school degrees climbed by about 53 percent, but obesity among college graduates jumped by 163 percent. If the "blame fast food" hypothesis made sense, these data would be flipped upside down.

Ritter. © 2002 by *Arizona Tribune*. Reproduced by permission of North America Syndicate.

Of course, we cannot deny that people are eating more and getting bigger, but that does not prove that fast food franchises are the culprit. On average, Americans are eating about 200 calories more each day than they did in the 1970s. An additional 200 calories can be guzzled in a glass of milk or a soda or gobbled in a bowl of cereal, for example. Fast food's critics eagerly pounce and allege that the additional calories come from super-sized meals of pizza, burgers, or burritos. It is true that between the 1970s and 1990s, daily fast food intake grew from an average of 60 calories to 200 calories. But simply quoting these data misleads. Though Americans have been consuming somewhat more fast food at mealtime, they have reduced their home consumption at mealtime. Americans have cut back their home meals by about 228 calories for men and 177 for women, offsetting the rise in fast food calories. In total, mealtime calories have not budged much, and mealtimes are when consumers generally visit fast food restaurants.

Snacking

So where are the 200 additional calories coming from? The U.S. Department of Agriculture (USDA) has compiled the "Continuing Survey of Food Intakes by Individuals," which collects information on where a food was purchased, how it was prepared, and where it was eaten, in addition to demographic information such as race, income, age, and sex. The survey shows that the answer is as close as the nearest salty treat. Americans are not eating bigger breakfasts, lunches, or dinners—but they are noshing and nibbling like never before. Between the 1970s and the 1990s, men and women essentially doubled the calories consumed between meals (by between 160 and 240 calories). In 1987–88, Americans typically snacked less than once a day; by 1994 they were snacking 1.6 times per day. But surely, opponents of fast food would argue, those cookies and pre-wrapped apple pies at McDonald's must account for calories. Again the data fail to make their case. Women ate only about six more snack calories at fast food restaurants, while men ate eight more snack calories, over the past two decades. That is roughly equal to one Cheez-It cracker or a few raisins. Where do Americans eat their between-meal calories? Mostly at home. Kitchen cabinets can be deadly to diets. And in a fairly recent development, supermarket shoppers are pulling goodies off of store shelves and ripping into them at the stores before they even drive home. Consumers eat two to three times more goodies inside stores than at fast food restaurants. . . .

Super-Sized Portions

Fast food's detractors also like to criticize portion sizes. True, fast-food restaurants have been offering super-sized sandwiches, drinks, and french fries. But have these critics been to a movie theater lately, where popcorn containers look like bushel baskets? Or to fancy restaurants featuring all-you-can-eat Sunday buffets? A study in the *Journal of the American Medical Association* (January 22, 2003) cited the "most surprising result [as] the large portion-size increases for food consumed at home—a shift that indicates marked changes in eating behavior in general." People eat bigger portions of hamburgers, fries, and Mexican food on their own kitchen tables than when they are sitting on a fast food restaurant stool. In the study, "Patterns and Trends in Food Portion Sizes, 1977–1988," researchers Samara J. Nielsen and Barry M. Popkin found that "the average home-cooked hamburger now weighs in at about 8 ounces, versus perhaps 5.5 ounces in full-service restaurants and a little over 7 ounces at fast-food outlets." When the USDA surveyed portion sizes and compared them to official U.S. government portions, they did find that fast food hamburgers exceeded official estimates by 112 percent. Yet they also found that Americans were eating pasta portions that surpass official measures by 333 percent and muffins that rise to 480 percent of the official sizes. If we are turning into a jumbo people, we are a jumbo people everywhere we eat, not just where the tort lawyers target defendants. . . .

Governing What We Eat

The Food and Drug Administration, with its battalion of researchers, aided by thousands of university and private-sector scientists throughout the world, is constantly exploring, testing, and digging for scientific insight. A class action lawsuit would not be digging for scientific inferences. Instead, plaintiffs' lawyers would be digging into the pockets of franchise owners, employees, and shareholders in order to pull out gold. Moreover, the threat of such lawsuits can do no good to the employees, shareholders, or customers of fast food firms. When tort lawyers strut in front of cameras waving weighty complaints that are flimsy in facts, the media quickly follow the story. Nearly every major publication in the country carried stories about the McDonald's obesity suit. If "McLawsuits" spread, we will see at least one, if not all, of the following three results: 1) lower wages for fast food employees; 2) lower stock prices for shareholders; 3) higher prices for consumers. Fast food restaurants hire and train hundreds of thousands of workers, attract investments from millions of middle-class citizens, and quench the hunger and thirst of tens of millions of satisfied patrons.

Let us be frank here. Depending on what you pile on it, a fast food burger may not enhance your health, and it may even hinder your ability to run a marathon—but it is very easy to find out how fatty that burger is. You do not need a lawyer by your side to pry open a brochure or to check the thousands of websites that will provide nutrition data. While it is unlikely that nutritionists will soon announce that super-sized double cheeseburgers will make you thin, society should not allow the latest fads or the most lucrative lawsuits to govern what we eat for lunch.

Periodical Bibliography

The following articles have been selected to supplement the diverse views presented in this chapter.

Kelly D. Brownell and David S. Ludwig	"Fighting Obesity and the Food Lobby," *Washington Post*, June 17–23, 2002.
Michael Fumento	"Big Fat Fake," *Reason*, March 2003.
Christine Gorman	"Desperate Measures: As a Last Resort, More and More Obese Teens Are Having Their Stomachs Stapled. What Are the Risks?" *Time*, November 17, 2003.
Jennifer Grossman	"The Perils of 'Fat Acceptance,'" *National Review*, November 24, 2003.
Bernadine Healy	"Rebuilding the Pyramid," *U.S. News & World Report*, September 6, 2004.
Issues and Controversies On File	"Fast-Food Litigation," December 13, 2002.
Patrick Johnson	"The Skinny on Fat: A Skeptical Evaluation of the Atkins and Other Low Carb Diets," *Skeptic*, Winter 2004.
David Limbaugh	"Beware of High-Fat Tort-Feasors," *Conservative Chronicle*, August 7, 2002.
Rosie Mestrel	"The Food Pyramid: Does It Miss the Point?" *Los Angeles Times*, September 1, 2000.
People Weekly	"Weighing the Risks: Gastric-Bypass Surgery Has Helped Thousands Defeat Obesity. But 'Stomach Stapling' Can Come with Serious—Even Deadly—Complications," March 10, 2003.
John C. Peters	"Social Change and Obesity Prevention: Where Do We Begin?" *Nutrition Today*, May/June 2004.
Stuart Reid	"I Give Up," *Spectator*, November 2, 2002.
Rob Stein	"Obesity Surgery Is Skyrocketing," *Washington Post*, April 19–25, 2004.
Claudia Wallis	"The Obesity Warriors: What Will It Take to End This Epidemic? These Experts Are Glad You Asked," *Time International*, August 9, 2004.

CHAPTER 4

Who Should Take Responsibility for Obesity?

Chapter Preface

In Landover, Maryland, Giant Food supermarket does not just sell food; it offers some other unusual services. The retailer has two dietitians on staff, and offers store tours and free nutrition advice to customers. Likewise, in Richmond, Virginia, at Ukrop's Super Market, the staff includes a manager of nutrition and wellness as well as three full-time and two part-time dietitians. The store also has a nutrition hotline. As obesity among Americans continues to increase, many grocers believe they can help address the problem by using their powerful influence to encourage people to purchase and eat more healthful food.

The many proponents of this strategy believe that not only can the supermarket industry play a role in preventing obesity, but it is obligated to do so. Kathleen Zelman, director of nutrition for the WebMD Weight Loss Clinic argues that grocery stores must be an important part of a nationwide effort to fight obesity because they have such a strong influence over what people eat. "It's going to take a village," she says. "It will require everyone's attention if we're going to stem the tide of this obesity epidemic." John Beckner, director of pharmacy and health services at Ukrop's, agrees that while supermarkets cannot force people to eat in a certain way, they are in an excellent position to educate and encourage people to eat more healthfully. "I think supermarkets have a responsibility," he says. "You can't preach to people, but you can offer healthy choices and healthy options, then let them make their own decision based on the information you give them."

However, many grocers contend that their role is merely to provide consumers with what food manufacturers produce, and that the responsibility for obesity lies with the manufacturers. According to researcher James E. Tillotson, the American food market is dominated by megacompanies that offer consumers less choice and more unhealthful food than ever before, thereby contributing to high rates of obesity. Researcher Marion Nestle agrees that grocery stores have a limited impact on obesity and that it is the food manufacturing industry that really needs to take action. "I think there are some things supermarkets can do, but it's complicated," she says. "It's not proven that these things will impact [the obesity epidemic]."

While most people agree that obesity is a serious problem that needs to be addressed, there is far less agreement on who should take responsibility for addressing it. The authors in the following chapter offer various opinions on this issue. The question of who is responsible for obesity has become increasingly contentious in countries such as the United States where obesity rates continue to rise steadily.

> "*Many people believe that dealing with
> . . . obesity is a personal responsibility. To
> some degree they are right, but it is also a
> community responsibility.*'"

Society Should Take Some Responsibility for Obesity

Morgan Downey

In the following viewpoint Morgan Downey argues that it is unfair to place the responsibility for obesity solely on the individual. He agrees that personal behavior does play a role in obesity. However, he points out, despite the role of individual choice, obesity is also a result of society's failure. For example, schools fail to provide healthy lunches to children and communities do not construct safe areas where people can exercise, he maintains. Downey is executive director of the American Obesity Association, an organization that works to change public policy and perceptions about obesity.

As you read, consider the following questions:
1. How does personal behavior play a role in the development of skin cancer, as explained by Downey?
2. According to David Satcher, as cited by the author, how is obesity a community responsibility?
3. In Downey's opinion, how is our reaction to obesity different from other diseases that are modifiable by personal behavior?

L ast week [February 2002] two reports crossed my desk. The first was a survey from the Grocery Manufacturers Association. It reported that 89% of Americans believe that individuals are to blame for being overweight. Only 5% thought that obesity was due to the environment or genetics.

The second report was that three homeless persons died in Washington last week during a cold spell in an otherwise unusually warm winter. The Mayor of Washington, D.C., Anthony Williams, was all over the news lamenting about the tragedy of the deaths of these homeless persons who escaped the District of Columbia's safety net.

A Simplistic Point of View

It does not take long in talking with politicians or health care policy persons to hear the refrain, "It's their fault." It is not surprising that 89% of the population, including, it must be assumed, many individuals who are overweight or obese, think their weight, is their own fault. But it is simplistic to leave the discussion there. Important questions remain:

- Is obesity among children their "fault"?
- Is our health care system based on "fault" in other areas?
- Does a fault-based approach help or hurt efforts to solve the problem?

So what is the picture about personal responsibility? How big is the issue of "personal responsibility" in obesity?

The scientists tell us that obesity is due to three primary factors (excluding specific diseases that cause obesity). They are (a) genetics (a predisposition to overweight), (b) environmental exposure to an energy-rich food supply and a tendency to reduction in physical activity and (c) personal behavior.

But most of the world, it seems, sees only personal behavior.

Accounting for Other Factors

Compare this to skin cancer or melanoma. For skin cancer (like obesity) three factors must be present. First, your genes give you fair skin. Second, you must have an environmental exposure to sunlight. Third, you must not take personal protective strategies, such as sunblockers, clothing, etc.

Now, if a person gets skin cancer no one says, "Don't treat them. They did it to themselves." No one says, "Melanoma is not a disease. They did it to themselves."

How many of us have had a parent or grandparent mistake the gas pedal for the brake pedal. Their car races across a few lanes in a mall and hits a light pole. They may have a broken wrist, maybe a head injury. People flock over to help. No one says, "Don't call 911. They did it to themselves."

What Communities Can Do

- Provide environmental inducements to physical activity, such as safe, accessible, and attractive trails for walking and bicycling, and sidewalks with curb cuts.

- Open schools for community recreation, form neighborhood watch groups to increase safety, and encourage malls and other indoor or protected locations to provide safe places for walking in any weather.

- Provide community-based programs to meet the needs of specific populations, such as racial and ethnic minority groups, women, older adults, persons with disabilities, and low-income groups.

- Encourage health care providers to talk routinely to their patients about incorporating physical activity into their lives.

- Encourage employers to provide supportive worksite environments and policies that offer opportunities for employees to incorporate moderate physical activity into their daily lives.

Chattanooga-Hamilton County Regional Health Council, November 2000.

How about sexually transmitted diseases, including HIV/AIDs? Does anyone say, "Let's not research this disease and let's not have prevention programs and let's not have insurance pay for treatment. They did it to themselves?" (Actually some people did say this about persons with HIV/AIDs but they lost the public debate.)

How about lung cancer and emphysema? Does anyone say. "Don't pay for lung cancer treatment. They did it to themselves." Of course not.

How about liver disease? Anyone say, "You drank too much. You did it to yourself. Insurance won't pay."

The fact is that many, many health care conditions are mediated by personal behavior. One third of all cancers are attributed to diet and lack of exercise. Does anyone say cancer is not a disease?

Our society responds by taking personal behavior into account and dealing with it through education. Except for obesity. For obesity it—personal behavior—is the end of the discussion. More money for research? Forget about it. Insurance coverage for treatment? Inyourdreams! Prevention? Getoffyourbutt!

Surgeon General David Satcher said it well in his Call to Action, "Many people believe that dealing with overweight and obesity is a personal responsibility. To some degree they are right, but it is also a community responsibility. When there are no safe, accessible places for children to play or adults to walk, jog, or ride a bike, that is a community responsibility. When school lunchrooms or office cafeterias do not provide health and appealing food choices, that is a community responsibility."

The Need for Compassion

For homeless persons who choose not to come to publicly supported shelter, for smokers who get lung cancer, for the sexually promiscuous who do not use protection, for sun worshippers who don't put on sunscreen, for all these persons our society in general and many of us personally we have compassion for these individuals in spite of the contribution personal behavior played in their disease. At least we acknowledge that there is a difference between their behavior and their disease. Except in obesity. Obesity is different. The moral judgement of laziness, lack of self-control, weakness even extend to denying obesity is a disease. Thus, obesity is not so different from other diseases which are modifiable by personal behavior. But our reaction to it is. Its principal feature may be that we suspend the compassion we normally feel. It is above all marked by this—the Suspension of Compassion.

"Obesity is a problem for many people, but it is not a public *health problem.*

Obesity Is Not Society's Responsibility

David Boaz

Obesity-related health problems are the result of personal choices and are thus not society's responsibility, maintains David Boaz in the following viewpoint. He believes that it is unfair to hold the public responsible for the health problems of the obese, and that attempts to do so are merely a result of government health agencies trying to broaden their influence and collect more taxes. Boaz is executive vice president of the Cato Institute, a public policy research foundation.

As you read, consider the following questions:
1. What did "public health" initially mean, as explained by the author?
2. What makes something a legitimate public health issue, according to Boaz?
3. In the author's opinion, what will be the result of calling obesity a public health problem?

David Boaz, "Obesity and Public Health?" www.cato.org, July 20, 2004. Copyright © 2004 by The Cato Institute. Reproduced by permission.

Health and Human Services Secretary Tommy Thompson says, "Obesity is a critical public health problem in our country."

Wrong. Obesity is a problem for many people, but it is not a *public* health problem. By calling it one, however, Thompson can promise that we, the taxpayers, will pay for everyone's diet programs, stomach surgery, and behavioral counseling. Get out your wallet.

The Concept of Public Health

The meaning of "public health" has sprawled out lazily over the decades. Once, it referred to the project of securing health benefits that were public: clean water, improved sanitation, and the control of epidemics through treatment, quarantine, and immunization. Public health officials worked to drain swamps that might breed mosquitoes and thus spread malaria. They strove to ensure that water supplies were not contaminated with cholera, typhoid, or other diseases. The U.S. Public Health Service began as the Marine Hospital Service, and one of its primary functions was ensuring that sailors didn't expose domestic populations to new and virulent illnesses from overseas.

Those were legitimate public health issues because they involved consumption of a collective good (air or water) and/or the communication of disease to parties who had not consented to put themselves at risk. It is difficult for individuals to protect themselves against illnesses found in air, water, or food. A breeding ground for disease-carrying insects poses a risk to entire communities.

Plenty of people in Africa and Asia still need those basic public health measures. As [writer] Jerry Taylor writes in *Regulation* magazine: "Diseases associated with inadequate sanitation, indoor air pollution from biomass stoves and furnaces, and contaminated water occur mainly in developing countries and account for 30 percent of the total burden of disease in those nations. Diarrheal diseases, brought on by poor sanitation and contaminated water, alone kill more than three million children annually, and experts believe that two million of those deaths could easily be prevented with even minimal improvements in sanitation and water quality. Approximately seven million die each year from conditions like tuberculosis, cholera, typhoid, and hookworm that could be inexpensively prevented and cured and are virtually unknown as serious health problems in advanced countries."

Looking for More Problems to Solve

In the United States and other developed countries those public health problems have been largely solved. For instance, in the 1920s there were 13,000–15,000 reported cases of diphtheria each year in the United States. Only one case was reported each year in 1998, 1999, and 2000. Before 1963, there were about 500,000 cases of measles and 500 measles deaths reported each year. A record low annual total of 86 cases was reported in 2000. The last cases of smallpox on earth occurred in an outbreak of two cases (one of which was fatal) in Birmingham, England in 1978, almost 30 years after the last case in the United States.

But bureaucracies are notoriously unwilling to become victims of their own success. So, true to form, the public health authorities broadened their mandate and kept on going. They launched informational and regulatory crusades against such health problems as smoking, venereal disease, AIDS and obesity. Pick up any newspaper and you're apt to find a story about these "public health crises." Those are all health problems, to be sure, but are they really *public* health problems?

There's an easy, perfectly private way to avoid increased risk of lung cancer and heart disease: Don't smoke. You don't need any collective action for that. Want to avoid AIDS and other sexually transmitted diseases? Don't have sex, or use condoms. (The threat to the blood supply did have public health aspects and was dealt with promptly.) As for obesity, it doesn't take a village for me to eat less and exercise more.

Not a Public Health Problem

Language matters. Calling something a "public health problem" suggests that it is different from a personal health problem in ways that demand collective action. And while it doesn't strictly follow, either in principle or historically, that "collective action" must be state action, that distinction is easily elided in the face of a "public health crisis." If smoking and obesity are called public health problems, then it seems that we need a public health bureaucracy to solve them—and the Public Health Service and all its sister agencies don't get to close up shop with the satisfaction of a job well done. So let's start using honest language: Smoking and obesity are health problems. In fact, they are *widespread* health problems. But they are not public health problems.

Secretary Thompson should not require the taxpayers to pay for individual behavioral choices. But maybe if our taxes go up enough, we won't be able to afford to overeat.

"Aggressive public health efforts must become the first line of defense [against obesity]."

The Government Should Take Action to Help Reduce Obesity

Ellen Ruppel Shell

According to Ellen Ruppel Shell in the following viewpoint, obesity is a public health problem that has a costly and devastating effect on society. She argues that the government must take action—through regulation and education—to counter the powerful negative influence that the food industry has on people's eating habits. Shell is codirector of the Knight Center for Science and Medical Journalism at Boston University and author of *The Hungry Gene: The Science of Fat and the Future of Thin.*

As you read, consider the following questions:

1. According to the author, what have scientists known for decades about obesity?
2. Why do public health messages such as "five a day" have little effect in countering obesity, as argued by Shell?
3. In the author's opinion, why might government subsidies of fruits and vegetables help reduce obesity?

Al Roker, the amiable "Today" show weatherman, and Rep. Jerrold Nadler, a Manhattan Democrat, recently revealed that they had undergone stomach-reduction surgery for their morbid obesity. They had struggled with obesity all their lives and had tried many remedies without success. So they each took extreme surgical measures because, like an increasing number of Americans, they saw no alternative.

A Public Health Disaster

Each year, obesity claims about 300,000 American lives and soaks up about $120 billion in health-care costs. Yet, as a nation, we have done almost nothing to combat it.

That Nadler's twin brother is also obese is not surprising. Scientists have known for decades that obesity has an important genetic component, a fact made irrefutable by the discovery of the obese gene at Rockefeller University in 1994. Subsequent research points to the increasing role of genetic factors.

Yet with more than 30% of Americans obese and fully two-thirds overweight, we continue to consider obesity a lifestyle choice rather than the public health disaster it has so clearly become.

Gastric bypass surgery is increasingly being performed on children, a practice whose potentially dangerous consequences are unknown. What we do know is that American children are becoming overweight and obese at an alarming rate, with fully 15% in the danger zone. As a consequence, obesity-linked disorders are increasingly common in the young, among them Type II diabetes, a devastating and costly disorder that until just a couple of decades ago was almost unheard of in children.

In "Illness as Metaphor," [writer] Susan Sontag wrote: "Any important disease whose causality is murky, and for which treatment is ineffectual, tends to be awash in significance." Obesity fits the bill. Mythology shrouding the disorder has muffled sensible discourse and, until the past decade, stymied research.

But in recent years, obesity science has exploded, offering startling new insights into the genetic, prenatal and environmental factors underlying body weight regulation. We now know that obesity is the consequence of environment acting on genetic inclination, and that genetic predisposition combined with an increasingly "obesegenic" environment underlies the current pandemic.

Government "Interference"

The idea that the government should decline to "interfere" in our "consumer preferences" is preposterous. Big business interferes the whole time, filling shops, pubs, restaurants and high-street takeaways with high-fat, sugar-rich junk food, and filling the media with propaganda to persuade us and our children to eat it.

New Statesman, May 31, 2004.

Some of us are more vulnerable to the environmental effects than others, but none of us is immune.

The Need to Counter Big Food

Anemic public service messages such as eat "five a day" (referring to servings of vegetables and fruits) do little to counter the temptations launched—and aggressively marketed—by a rabidly competitive processed-food industry.

Big Food is a cunning manipulator of public opinion, characterizing its critics as a conspiracy of "food cops, vegetarian activists and meddling bureaucrats" intent on using "junk science" to build a "nanny state."

But eating decisions, like all decisions, are molded by available information. Advertising is by far the most potent source of information when it comes to food. It's time to counter industry influence with a vigorous public information campaign based on the new science of appetite regulation.

Big Food argues that Americans are free to make healthy food choices, knowing full well that its incessant and cleverly designed messages are dissuading a growing number of us from doing so.

In the last decade, the restaurant and processed-food industries have increased substantially the sugar and fat load of their offerings. Cheap fat and sweeteners bulk up portion sizes, giving the perception of value at very low cost to producers. The marketing of these products, especially to children, has grown from vigorous to relentless.

Scientists now believe that eating large quantities of fat and sweeteners may—for at least some—muffle biochemical signals that tell the brain when we have eaten enough and that this effect is magnified by a sedentary lifestyle. This effect is probably genetically mediated, and some of us will feel the brunt of it more than others.

But as the food supply becomes increasingly rich, and our lives increasingly sedentary, more and more of us will have difficulty regulating our appetites and controlling our weight.

Government Regulation

By regulating food advertising to children and subsidizing the production of fruits, vegetables and other unprocessed foods, government could go far toward reversing this vicious cycle; studies make clear that all of us make food choices based partially on cost.

Obesity is not just an individual problem but a tragedy of the commons. Getting a grip on this costly pandemic will require making tough personal choices, certainly, but also tough public ones. Aggressive public health efforts must become the first line of defense. It is time for public servants such as Rep. Nadler to make the personal political.

*"The last thing we need is more
government intervention in our digestive
systems."*

The Government Should Not Take Action to Reduce Obesity

Robert E. Wright

In the following viewpoint Robert E. Wright disagrees with
the idea that government regulation is an effective way to reduce obesity. In his opinion, what an individual eats is entirely under his or her control, and government regulation
of food is unneeded and unwise. According to Wright, history shows that the government is not a reliable source of information about diet. Any action it takes to regulate what
people eat is unlikely to reduce obesity, he contends. Wright
is the author of *Wealth of Nations Rediscovered*.

As you read, consider the following questions:
1. Why might the government be likely to subsidize, tax,
   and restrict the wrong foods, according to Wright?
2. How does the author refute Ellen Ruppel Shell's claim
   that food advertisers influence people through
   advertising?
3. What is the main cause of the obesity pandemic,
   according to Wright?

M any Americans are overweight, Ellen Ruppel Shell, author of *The Hungry Gene*, reminded *Los Angeles Times* readers last Thanksgiving Day [2002] ("Big Food Has Become a Big Problem: Politicians and Health Officials Must Address Pandemic Obesity"). Her solution? More government regulation.

Shell calls for government to regulate food advertising to children and to subsidize the production of fruits and vegetables, hoping to increase the quantity demanded by driving down the price. Following that logic, a prohibitive sin tax on sugar and fat would be certain to follow. In short, Shell calls on the state to use its coercive powers to force Americans to eat what she believes is healthy.

Problems with Shell's Argument

The problems with Shell's program are numerous and deep. For starters, she apparently has little understanding of political economy. The government has already tried prohibiting alcohol and other drugs, restricting advertising of alcohol and tobacco, imposing sin taxes, and subsidizing agriculture. The results have been mixed—at best. Success here appears even less likely.

Moreover, scientists still do not understand the relationship between diet, weight, and health. The low-fat, high-carbohydrate regime many pushed for years has not worked; some have finally begun to take a serious look at low-carb, high-protein, and high-fat alternatives, such as the Atkins diet. Similarly, the received wisdom about the alleged link between cholesterol and heart disease has come under increased criticism of late. The foundation of modern nutritional and health theory has been shaken and the entire edifice may soon tumble down. However, it may take many more years, even decades, before we learn the Truth about diet. In the meantime, if politicians follow Shell's advice, they may subsidize, tax, and restrict the wrong foods.

The biggest problem with Shell's article, however, is her limited understanding of human behavior. She formulaically asserts that "obesity is the consequence of environment acting on genetic inclination, and that genetic predisposition combined with an increasingly 'obesegenic' environment underlies the current pandemic." According to Shell, Americans are passive victims of two forces beyond their immediate control, their genetic makeup and the "obesegenic" environment in which they live. Americans cannot change their genes, but they can, with the help of Big Brother government, make the environment less conducive to obesity. That is old statist rhetoric with a bone thrown to genetic determinists. The missing element, of course, is human volition, good old free will.

Individual Control

You see, human beings are endowed with the wonderful ability to think, to reason, to make decisions for themselves. They must work within the constraints set by genetics and environment, but can pick from innumerable remaining possible choices. For instance, without the aid of technology, I am genetically incapable of flying or of burrowing very far into the earth. But I can choose whether to run, jog, skip, walk, crawl, or crabwalk to get around.

Similarly, I could not live on a diet composed entirely of mercury or of twigs, but there are vast combinations of foods in between that are *entirely under my control*. (As Shell notes, Americans are bombarded with food advertisements. But advertisers should not be able to rule us, and to the extent that they do, it is because the government's schools do an inadequate job of teaching critical thinking.)

Americans need to know that in the vast majority of cases, *they decide* whether they will be overweight, just as they decide whether they will use tobacco, alcohol, or other drugs. But they have been given bad information on which to base their decisions. Blaming obesity on a "fat gene" or the alleged evils of "Big Food" will only exacerbate the problem by directing attention away from the main cause of the "pandemic," government meddling. This is yet another case of statists using *government failures* as excuses to call for yet more regulation. Instead of allowing Americans to make their own food choices, the government leveraged its control of the educational system and scientific establishment to inculcate impressible Americans with the notion that to be healthy they had to eat lots of starches and sugars and little fat or protein. That diet left Americans feeling hungry, so they loaded

Asay. © 2002 by Creators Syndicate. Reproduced by permission.

up on more bread, pasta, and starchy vegetables instead of the fat and protein their bodies needed and craved. We know the result.

Government Doesn't Know

So, at this point the last thing we need is more government intervention in our digestive systems. What is needed is the simple admission that scientists do not know everything about diet and that a little knowledge is a dangerous thing. Americans need to be told to forget everything they have "learned" about diet and health over the last few decades and to search out the diet that best suits their individual needs. A good place to start might be the various evolutionary diets like the *Dr. Atkins' New Diet Revolution, The Paleo Diet,* and *Neanderthin.* Such diets have the virtue of being based on the foods that humans thrived on for millions of years. From what we can gather from archeological and ethnographic evidence, our hunter-gatherer ancestors were fine physical specimens, neither gaunt nor obese.

Moreover, those who study ancient human diets make a number of interesting points that vitiate many of Shell's assumptions. For example, they note that today's fruits and vegetables have been domesticated to contain much higher levels of sugar and starch than their counterparts found in nature. Anyone who has ever tasted a "wild" apple will immediately appreciate that point. But again, scientists do not know much about the relationship between diet, weight, or health more generally. Our ancestral diet is a good place for modern Americans to start, but it may not be the place to end. The key point is that individuals should be encouraged to find what works best for them, as individuals. Al Roker and others who opted for stomach-staple surgery may have found that increasing their fat intake would have curbed their appetites and allowed them to lose weight and keep it off without resort to the staple gun.

Competing Interests

That brings me to my final point. Clearly, there are a large number of competing economic interests at play here. Are stomach staplers and producers of diet drugs upset about our bulging waistlines? Do heart surgeons really want to reduce coronary heart disease? What about pharmaceutical companies? If a major study concluded that red meat is good for us after all, would pork suddenly become the "other red meat"? Do the left-leaning media really want to give [Robert] Atkins [creator of the Atkins diet] and his followers full exposure? Does the government have an incentive to keep Americans fat and hence (seemingly) dependent on government entitlement programs like Medicare? Given all those conflicting economic interests, can Truth ever clearly emerge and enjoy wide dissemination? Yes, I believe, if government allows health-insurance companies to take the lead. Private insurers have both the resources and the incentives to discover and disseminate the Truth. They also have the power, through premium differentials, to induce Americans to listen.

"We need a movement that effectively challenges the capitalist entities that push their interests no matter the weight or health effects."

Much of the Responsibility for Obesity Lies with Corporations

Yves Engler

In the following viewpoint Yves Engler claims that American corporations have played a major role in the escalating obesity epidemic. She cites aggressive advertising by fast food companies and the transformation of the urban landscape by automobile manufacturers into car-friendly, pedestrian-hostile environments as examples of how companies have encouraged overeating and underexercising. In her opinion, attempts to combat obesity must involve these irresponsible companies. Engler is a Montreal-based activist.

As you read, consider the following questions:
1. What is the main reason that people are eating more, according to Engler?
2. As cited by the author, what percentage of McDonald's advertising targets children?
3. Why did the World Health Organization and the United Nations back down on sugar consumption guidelines, as explained by Engler?

Yves Engler, "The Obesity Epidemic: The Business Opportunities in Obesity," *Z Magazine*, vol. 16, December 2003. Copyright © 2003 by Yves Engler. Reproduced by permission.

In early October [2003] there was a quirky report about U.S. coffin makers increasing the size of their product. What this reveals is anything but funny. Obesity is one of today's biggest health crises—1 in 4 of the world's 4 billion adults are overweight and 300 million are clinically obese. In the U.S., where the crisis is most pronounced, nearly a third of the population is obese and two-thirds overweight, with the rates substantially higher among the poor. Since 1990 the U.S. obesity rate has doubled and approximately 127 million adults are now overweight and 60 million are obese. During the same period the number of people who are severely obese has nearly quadrupled to nine million. Child obesity is also increasing rapidly.

A Serious Problem

Outside the U.S., especially in the more advanced capitalist nations, obesity is also skyrocketing. In Canada between 1985 and 2001, the prevalence of obesity more than doubled from 7 percent to 14 percent among women and to 16 percent from 6 percent among men. Like the U.S., the rates are substantially higher among the poor. According to a study published in the August [2003] edition of the *International Journal of Obesity*, 6.4 percent of children in the wealthiest quarter of the population compared with 12.8 percent of those in the poorest quarter are obese.

The health effects of the obesity epidemic are immense. Researchers claim there are links between obesity and more than 30 medical conditions including heart disease, diabetes, hypertension, cancers, and possibly Alzheimers. According to the Centers for Disease Control and Prevention, 1 in 3 U.S. children—nearly 50 percent of black and Latino children—born in 2000 will become diabetic unless people start exercising more and eating less. Some 90,000 U.S. cancer deaths a year are linked to obesity. Worldwide, diet-related afflictions such as heart disease, hypertension, and diabetes account for almost 60 percent of deaths annually.

Even in crude economic terms obesity is costly. The U.S. National Institutes of Health estimates that the annual costs of treating obesity-related conditions are at least $120 billion. . . .

Changing Diets

Throughout the advanced capitalist world, and to a lesser extent in the periphery, people's diets have changed drastically over the past 30 years. In the U.S., spending on fast food now totals $110 billion annually, having increased 18-fold since 1970. The number of fast food outlets, often started with government subsidies, has doubled from 1 per 2,000 residents to 1 in 1,000 since 1980. Poor areas often have an even higher exposure to fast food restaurants and fewer supermarkets, four times less in black neighborhoods than white neighborhoods, where healthier products can be found (even though there is evidence that supermarkets in poorer neighborhoods are more profitable per square foot). Outside the U.S., fast food restaurants are also rapidly expanding. For instance, in 1995 Dunkin' Donuts opened 1,000 international stores, which by 2000 had increased to 5,000.

It's not only at fast food restaurants where unhealthy products are being consumed in greater quantities. U.S. residents on average consume an astounding 848—2.3 per day—8-ounce servings of soft drinks annually. In poorer countries people are also increasingly consuming high calorie soda pop instead of more nutritious drinks. The Mexican soft drink market, 70 percent controlled by Coca-Cola, totals some 633 eight-ounce servings per person annually.

Portion sizes have also expanded. Compared with 20 years ago U.S. hamburger servings have increased by 112 percent, bagels 195 percent, steaks 224 percent, muffins 333 percent, pasta 480 percent, and chocolate chip cookies 700 percent. It has been shown that people consume about 30 percent more when served larger portions. Fast food outlets and the rest of the food industry often promote their products based on their larger, somehow more empowering, size. As of 1996, a quarter of the $97 billion spent on fast food came from items promoted on the basis of either extra size or larger portions.

Relentless Advertising

The main reason that people are consuming more, especially unhealthy products, is the food industry's relentless advertising, especially to children. U.S. food companies spend more than $30 billion to sell their products, not counting what they spend lobbying favorable policies and support. In 2001, Coca-Cola and Pepsi together spent $3 billion in advertising.

When targeting young kids, companies use cartoon characters, toys, and other items that have a powerful influence over children. In the early 1970s the U.S. food industry fought off regulation of their advertising practices and instead adopted industry-regulated standards—the Children's Advertising Review Unit. Now 40 percent of McDonald's advertising targets children and, according to a 1998 study, they've been highly successful. Of 10,000 children surveyed, 100 percent of U.S., 98 percent of Japanese, and 93 percent of UK children recognized Ronald McDonald, with many of these kids believing Ronald McDonald knows what's best for their health.

The fast food and soft drink companies have also been successful at getting their products into cash-strapped schools. They get ad spots on Channel One, which is shown in classes. In Texas, the food giants give $54 million a year to schools to sell their wares in vending machines. Maybe the most disturbing example of school infiltration was in 1998 when Colorado Springs school officials agreed to an exclusive agreement with Coke, based on a tripling of school soft drink sales. Recently Coca-Cola Enterprises became an official sponsor of the PTA [Parent-Teacher Association] and John H. Downs Jr., the company's senior vice president for public affairs and chief lobbyist, got a seat on the PTA's board.

Influencing Regulatory Agencies

The food interests are also hard at work lobbying governments, both behind the scenes and with front groups such as the Center for Consumer Freedom. Three years ago [2000] sugar producers and the soft drink industry won a big victory in getting the USDA [U.S. Department of Agriculture] to soften its dietary guidelines on sugar. Likewise, they convinced a subservient American Dietetic Association to refrain from labeling any foods as unhealthy since according to them, "all foods can fit into a healthy eating style."

Last September [2002], within a week of the European Commission strengthening regulations on companies promoting the health benefits of foods high in fat and sugars, the Food and Drug Administration weakened its guidelines to allow food packages to advertise possible benefits before they are fully approved. Currently, different sectors of the food industry are hard at work shaping changes to the New Food Pyramid.

The "Triumph" of Capitalism

The fast food industry began as a triumph of capitalism but it has slowly degraded into one of the worst causes of obesity, poverty and homogenization in America.

According to a recent study by the Centers for Disease Control and Prevention [CDC], approximately 64 percent of Americans are either overweight or obese. The growth of the fast food industry strongly correlates with this increase.

The gene pool has not changed much in the recent past, which leads to one conclusion: Americans are eating more and moving less. Obesity has grown at such alarming rates that the CDC has declared it an epidemic.

Evan Goldin, http://voice.paly.net, December 6, 2002.

Internationally a similar process is at work. This past April [2003] the World Health Organization (WHO) and the UN [United Nations] food and agricultural organization [FAO] backed down (due to pressure from the sugar industry) on guidelines, stating that people should limit daily consumption of free sugars to a maximum of 10 percent of energy intakes to avoid chronic diseases. U.S. sugar producers had indicated that they may lobby the Bush administration and Congress to link U.S. funding—about one-fifth of the WHO budget—to changes in research methods at the UN agency.

The food giants are well represented in other ways. In 1978 Coca-Cola, Pepsi-Cola, Kraft, and other food companies founded the International Life Sciences Institute (ILSI) to lobby WHO. It won a position as an NGO [nongovernmental organization] "in official relations" with WHO and a specialized consultative status with the Food and Agricultural Organization in 1991. In 1992 the ILSI congratulated themselves after steering the WHO and FAO away from any curbs on sugar consumption.

The 10 percent or 200-calorie increase in energy consumption by the average U.S. resident over the past 25 years is tied to incessant food advertising, political lobbying, and larger portions. Underlying this rise, however, is an agricultural sector that has increased output by some 500 calories per person during this period—after the Nixon administration altered government subsidies effectively increasing farmers incentives to expand their yields. . . .

The Effects of Automation

Workplaces and their power struggles also affect obesity. The automation of work reduces the amount of energy workers expend. In and of itself this needn't be problematic since automation should also reduce the number of hours worked and increase time for active leisure; not in the U.S., where people are working 200 hours a year more than they did in the early 1970s.

According to Linda Rosenstock, the former Director of the National Institute for Occupational Safety and Health, "It turns out that a quarter to a third of workers have high job stress and are drained and used up at the end of the day." Thus, many working people have less time to take part in activities. In addition, after a long day's work, people often turn to TV watching, which is inversely linked to time spent exercising. Busy parents, especially poor working class people, use TV as a babysitter. In this setting children who are naturally active are hindered from activity.

Often the same automation technology, which is supposed to reduce the workload, results in an increased workload (stress level) for those who retain their jobs. A growing body of evidence shows that workers who don't feel in control of their work environment have higher job stress levels. Scientists believe there is a link between stress and the impulse to eat. Food with lots of sugar, fat, and calories appear literally to calm down the body's response to chronic stress. In addition, research indicates that stress hormones encourage the formation of fat cells, particularly the kind that are the most dangerous to health.

The Role of Urban Planning

Oddly enough a historical determinant in work related stress —repetitive assembly line work—has also contributed to obesity in another way. Urban planning, which is intimately linked to the expansion of capital, plays a central role in obesity. How the suburban landscape became the norm is told, in part, by Colleen Fuller in *Caring for Profit*. "Beginning in the 1920s, General Motors [GM] president Alfred Sloan and top company executives masterminded a scheme to create a consumer market for automobiles in the United States. At the time, 9 out of 10 people relied on the trolley networks that criss-crossed cities across the country. GM first purchased and then dismantled the nation's trolley companies, ripping up tracks and setting bonfires composed of railcars. In 30 short years GM succeeded in destroying a mass-transit infrastructure that would cost many billions of dollars to resurrect—more money than municipal governments could raise."

It's not just the auto industry (broadly defined) that has re-organized cities in a way that encourages obesity. Land developers are notorious for buying up cheap agricultural land on the outskirts of cities and pushing for land rezoning and the extension of public amenities to these plots. There is substantially more money to be made from selling houses or commercial space than there is in harvesting vegetables. Similarly, today in many towns Wal-Mart has played no small role in undermining the downtown core, one of the only places where people regularly walked.

The suburban landscape is almost entirely subservient to the car. Sidewalks are non-existent or disconnected, cross-walks are absent or poorly marked, and the speed and volume of vehicular traffic is overwhelming, which makes walking or biking either impractical or dangerous. So people who might otherwise walk are forced to drive even short distances and kids who could easily walk to school must be chauffeured.

A study released in September [2003] showed that in the 25 most sprawling U.S. counties people were on average 6 pounds heavier than in the 25 most compact counties. In the past 20 years the number of trips taken on foot in the U.S. has dropped by 42 percent. Now, fewer than 10 percent of children walk or bike to school regularly, down from 66 percent 30 years ago.

Challenging Capitalist Forces

To combat the obesity epidemic we need tighter limits on fast food marketing. Junk food companies should be kicked out of schools. Perhaps governments should subsidize fruits and vegetables as well as other healthy products. Increased funding for physical education classes, park spaces, and children's sports would help. Increasing exercise opportunities at work, which a group of large employers, ironically headed by Ford Motors and Pepsi Co., is already working on, could help. Also there could be some form of tax break for exercise as is the case in Finland where some 70 percent of the population exercises for 30 minutes 5 times a week.

Most important we need a movement that effectively challenges the capitalist entities that push their interests no matter the weight or health effects.

"We cannot continue to blame any one industry or any one restaurant for the nation's obesity epidemic."

The Responsibility for Obesity Lies with the Individual

Gerard J. Musante

In the following viewpoint, originally given as congressional testimony before the Senate's Subcommittee on Administrative Oversight and the Courts on October 16, 2003, Gerard J. Musante emphasizes the role that individual responsibility plays in reducing obesity. According to Musante, food companies and other businesses do have an important impact on obesity levels; however, blaming these companies is not an effective way to reduce obesity. Ultimately, says Musante, obesity is due to individual choices, and the best way to reduce it is to help people make better decisions about diet and exercise. Musante is the founder of Structure House, a weight loss and lifestyle change clinic in Durham, North Carolina.

As you read, consider the following questions:
1. According to Musante, what will be the only result of lawsuits against the food industry?
2. Why is blaming outside forces the worst thing obese people can do, as argued by the author?
3. In Musante's opinion, which "players" in the obesity epidemic should be brought together in an obesity summit?

Gerard J. Musante, testimony before the U.S. Senate Subcommittee on Administrative Oversight and the Courts, Committee on the Judiciary, October 16, 2003.

I have been called here to share my expertise and educated opinion on the importance of personal responsibility in food consumption in the United States. This lesson is one I have been learning about and teaching for more than 30 years to those who battle moderate to morbid obesity—a lesson that emphasizes the criticality of taking responsibility for one's own food choices. I am testifying before [the Senate] because I am concerned about the direction in which today's obesity discourse is headed. We cannot continue to blame any one industry or any one restaurant for the nation's obesity epidemic. Instead, we must work together as a nation to address this complex issue, and the first step is to put the responsibility back into the hands of individuals.

A Unique Understanding of Obesity

As a clinical psychologist with training at Duke University Medical Center [North Carolina] and The University of Tennessee, I have worked for more than 30 years with thousands of obese patients. I have dedicated my career to helping Americans fight obesity. My personal road, which included the loss and maintenance of 50 of my own pounds, began when I undertook the study of obesity as a faculty member in the Department of Psychiatry at Duke University Medical Center. There, I began developing an evidenced-based, cognitive-behavioral approach to weight loss and lifestyle change. I continue to serve Duke University Medical Center as a Consulting Professor in the Department of Psychiatry. Since the early 1970's, I have published research studies on obesity and have made presentations at conferences regarding obesity and the psychological aspects of weight management.

Today [2003], I continue my work at Structure House—a residential weight loss facility in Durham, North Carolina—where participants come from around the country and the world to learn about managing their relationship with food. Participants lose significant amounts of weight while both improving various medical parameters and learning how to control and take responsibility for their own food choices. Our significant experience at Structure House has provided us with a unique understanding of the national obesity epidemic.

Some of the lessons I teach my patients are examples of

how we can encourage Americans to take personal responsibility for health and weight maintenance. As I tell my participants, managing a healthy lifestyle and a healthy weight certainly are not easy to do. Controlling an obesity or weight problem takes steadfast dedication, training and self-awareness. Therefore, I give my patients the tools they need to eventually make healthy food choices as we best know it. Nutrition classes, psychological understanding of their relationship with food, physical fitness training and education are tools that Structure House participants learn, enabling them to make sensible food choices.

As you know, the obesity rates in this country are alarming. The Centers for Disease Control and Prevention have recognized obesity and general lack of physical fitness as the nation's fastest-growing health threat. Approximately 127 million adults in the United States are overweight, 60 million are obese and 9 million are severely obese. The country's childhood obesity rates are on a similar course to its adult rates, as well as increases in type II diabetes. Fortunately, Americans are finally recognizing the problem. Unfortunately, many are taking the wrong approaches to combating this issue.

The Food Industry Is Not to Blame

Lawsuits are pointing fingers at the food industry in an attempt to curb the nation's obesity epidemic. These lawsuits do nothing but enable consumers to feel powerless in a battle for maintaining one's own personal health. The truth is, we as consumers have control over the food choices we make, and we must issue our better judgment when making these decisions. Negative lifestyle choices cause obesity, not a trip to a fast food restaurant or a cookie high in trans fat. Certainly we live in a litigious society. Our understanding of psychological issues tells us that when people feel frustrated and powerless, they lash out and seek reasons for their perceived failure. They feel the victim and look for the deep pockets to pay. Unfortunately, this has become part of our culture, but the issue is far too comprehensive to lay blame on any single food marketer or manufacturer. These industries should not be demonized for providing goods and services demanded by our society.

Rather than assigning blame, we need to work together toward dealing effectively with obesity on a national level. Furthermore, if we were to start with one industry, where would we stop? For example, a recent article in the *Harvard Law Review* suggests that there is a link between obesity and "preference manipulation," which means advertising. Should we consider suing the field of advertising next? Should we do away with all advertising and all food commercials at half time? We need to understand that this is a multi-faceted problem and there are many influences that play a part.

A Problem with Many Causes

While our parents, our environment, social and psychological factors all impact our food choices, can we blame them for our own poor decisions as it relates to our personal health and weight? For example, a recent study presented at the American Psychological Association conference showed that when parents change how the whole family eats and offer children wholesome rewards for not being couch potatoes, obese children shed pounds quickly. Should we bring lawsuits against parents that don't provide this proper direction? Similarly, Brigham and Women's Hospital in Boston recently reported in *Pediatrics* that children who diet may actually gain weight in the long run, perhaps because of metabolic changes, but also likely because they resort to binge eating as a result of the dieting. Do we sue the parent for permitting their children to diet?

From an environmental standpoint, there are still more outside influences that could be erroneously blamed for the nation's obesity epidemic. The Center for Disease Control has found that there is a direct correlation between television watching and obesity among children. The more TV watched, the more likely the children would be overweight. Should we sue the television industry, the networks, cable, the television manufacturers or the parents that permit this? And now we have internet surfing and computer games. Where does it stop?

School systems are eliminating required physical education—are we to also sue the school systems that do not require these courses?

How to Maintain a Healthy Weight

INTAKE	OUTPUT
Calories from Foods	Calories Used During Physical Activity

THE ENERGY BALANCE

U.S. Department of Health and Human Services, 2004.

Throw social influences into the mix and we have a whole new set of causes for obesity. Another recent study in *Appetite* indicated that social norms can affect quantitative ratings of internal states such as hunger. This means that other people's hunger levels around us can affect our own eating habits. Are we to blame the individuals who are eating in our presence for our own weight problems?

The Importance of Personal Responsibility

As evidenced in these studies, we cannot blame any one influencing factor for the obesity epidemic that plagues our nation. Through working with obese patients, I have learned that the worst thing one can do is to blame an outside force to get themselves "off the hook," to say it's not their fault, and that they are a victim. To do this can bring about feelings of helplessness and then resignation. Directing blame or causality outside of oneself allows the individual not to accept responsibility and perhaps even to feel helpless and hopeless. "The dog ate my homework" and "the devil made me do it" allows the individual not to take serious steps toward correction because they believe these steps are not within their power. We must take personal responsibility for our choices.

What does it mean to take personal responsibility for food consumption? It means making food choices that are not detrimental to your health, and not blaming others for the choices we make.

Ultimately, Americans generally become obese by taking in more calories than they expend. But certainly there are an increasing number of reasons why Americans are doing so producing rising obesity rates. Some individuals lack self-awareness and overindulge in food ever more so because of psychological reasons. Others do not devote enough time to physical activity, which becomes increasingly difficult to do in our society. Others lack education or awareness as it relates to nutrition and/or physical activity particularly in view of lessened exposure to this information. And still others may have a more efficient metabolism or hormonal deficiencies. In short, honorable members of the Subcommittee, there is yet much to learn about this problem.

No More Lawsuits

Congress has rightly recognized the danger of allowing Americans to continue blaming others for the obesity epidemic. It is imperative that we prevent lawsuits from being filed against any industry for answering consumer demands. The fact that we are addressing the issue here today is a step in the right direction. No industry is to blame and should not be charged with solving America's obesity problem.

Rather than pointing fingers, we should be working together on a national level to address the importance of personal responsibility in food consumption. The people who come to Structure House have a unique opportunity to learn these lessons, but they are only a select few. These lessons need to be encouraged on a national level, from an early age —in schools, homes and through national legislation that prevents passing this responsibility onto the food or other related industries.

In closing, I'd like to highlight the fact that personal responsibility is one of the key components that I teach my patients in their battle against obesity. This approach has allowed me to empower more than 10,000 Americans to embrace improved health. I urge you to consider how this type of approach could affect the obesity epidemic on a national level. By encouraging Americans to take personal responsibility for their health by limiting frivolous lawsuits against the food industry, we can put the power back into the hands of the consumers. This is a critical first step on the road toward addressing our nation's complex obesity epidemic.

"Public schools must take a big share of responsibility for the current epidemic of childhood obesity."

Schools Should Play a Role in Fighting Childhood Obesity

Phyllis Schlafly

In the following viewpoint Phyllis Schlafly maintains that rather than contributing to childhood obesity by providing easy access to junk foods and sodas, schools must take action to reduce it. In her opinion, schools exert a powerful influence over what children eat and the amount of time they spend exercising, and could thus be a powerful force in fighting obesity. Schlafly is a leader of the conservative movement in the United States. She writes a syndicated column that appears in one hundred newspapers, and her radio commentaries are heard daily on hundreds of stations.

As you read, consider the following questions:

1. According to Schlafly, what percentage of middle schools and high schools sell sodas in vending machines?
2. Why do corporations look upon schoolchildren as very profitable, in the author's opinion?
3. How does Florida's Fresh-2-U program encourage healthy eating among schoolchildren, as explained by Schlafly?

Phyllis Schlafly, "Fat Kids: Who's Responsible?" www.eagleforum.org, September 17, 2003. Copyright © 2003 by Phyllis Schlafly. Reproduced by permission.

Too many of our kids are too fat, so there ought to be a law. Turn the trial lawyers loose to blame the restaurants and the fast-food joints and give them the tobacco treatment. Right?

As with many other problems in our society today, the government may not be the solution, but it could be part of the problem.

Recent studies show that eleven percent of American children and adolescents are obese, and one in three is overweight. They face a costly future as obese adults, plagued by heart disease, high cholesterol levels, several types of cancer, and type II diabetes (which has risen 50 percent in the last ten years).

An Obesity-Friendly Environment

So why are we allowing public schools to impose an obesity-friendly environment on all students, even on those who come from homes where calorie-laden eatables are not allowed? Why do we permit schools to provide easy availability of junk foods, sodas, snacks and sweets from vending machines, and non-nutritious school lunches?

Why? Follow the money. These foods are big money-makers, and the schools get their cut from the profits. Nine out of ten U.S. schools now run lucrative a la carte programs at lunchtime. A la carte is French for selling kids sodas and junk foods as alternatives to school lunches.

Sodas from vending machines are sold in at least 60 percent of all middle schools and high schools, and the Texas statistics released by the state's Agriculture Commissioner are probably typical. With a majority of school districts responding to the survey, 52 percent had exclusive vending contracts with drink and food companies (63 percent of those contracts with Coca-Cola and 15 percent with Pepsi).

A study of Minneapolis-St. Paul-area schools published in the *American Journal of Public Health* tactfully described 93 percent of the a la carte foods sold to students as "foods to limit." In the schools where they were sold, students ate fewer fruits and vegetables and consumed more calories from fat and saturated fat than health guidelines stipulate.

Public schools must take a big share of responsibility for

the current epidemic of childhood obesity, not only because of the kinds of food and drinks they sell or give away, but because of the inducements that flow from easy availability and peer pressure. Of course, parents can't be excused from responsibility, but it's unrealistic to say it's the parents' job to forbid their children to eat, drink or buy what the schools provide.

Schools as Endorsers

Schools have a financial interest in promoting soda consumption because many receive a percentage of sales and/or have negotiated fees contingent on meeting sales quotas. Such arrangements encourage schools to aggressively promote these items. Vending machines have now become a principal source of extra money for districts across the nation, bringing in hundreds of millions of dollars for extracurricular activities each year. Money generated from the sale of junk food and sodas helps pay for sports equipment, after-school activities, field trips, and computers.

Schools also play a prominent role in exposing children to advertisements promoting fast foods, candy, and soda. An example is Channel One, an MTV-like show that reaches about eight million junior high and high school students in about 12,000 schools. Schools are lured with the promise of free television equipment. On this channel, ten-minute "news" segments are followed by two-minute commercials. When a school contractually obligates to Channel One, they commit to showing Channel One on 90 percent of school days each year. This amounts to one entire school day per year doing nothing but watching television advertising for products such as M & Ms, Snickers, Pepsi, and Mountain Dew.

Tonia Van Staveren and Darren Dale, *Journal of Physical Education, Recreation & Dance*, September 2004.

Where are the anti-prayer-in-schools and anti-pledge-of-allegiance lawyers who argue the right of atheist children not to be embarrassed in front of their peers? We could use their help to protect the health of schoolchildren who don't want to be embarrassed by the school-sponsored inducements to eat and drink unhealthy foods and sodas.

Schools have become a major marketing venue for companies, even more important than direct advertising. Yet there's been no public debate, or even a debate within the education community, about the adverse effects of commercializing childhood or about making kids pay with obesity for their school's profits from vending machines and a la carte menus.

A Captive Market

Corporations look upon schoolchildren as a very profitable market because even elementary schoolchildren have an estimated $15 billion of their own money and may influence $160 billion in parental purchases. The school administrators who sign the million-dollar contracts (without, of course, approval from parents), serve up the schoolchildren as a captive market to the corporations.

Parents who want their children to eat better can send them to school with a lunch bag from home. But (and here comes peer pressure again) surveys show that teenagers who bring a lunch usually trade it or put it in the trash.

Encouraging Healthy Eating and Exercise

Some local campaigns are beginning to take unhealthy foods out of schools. Palm Beach County, Florida has inaugurated a program called Fresh-2-U that encourages students to try 20 different fresh fruits and vegetables during the school year.

This program comes with coloring pages, posters, and music videos about the produce to appeal to the MTV generation. Report cards for fifth graders will tally their fruit and vegetable consumption.

Fresh-2-U is also improving the nutritional quality of school lunches and adding a dozen "healthy" vending machines in middle and high school. New machine-dispensing items will include tuna, milk and yogurt.

The exercise component of a get-trim regimen for kids may prove more difficult. Only 8 percent of elementary schools in Palm Beach County have daily recess.

The elimination of recess is one of the trendy policies imposed on schoolchildren by the feminists who want to make little boys behave like little girls. Eliminating recess gets rid of masculine games such as cops and robbers.

"A child learns . . . food rules and how much to eat in their environment which is largely 'controlled' by parents."

Parents Should Play a Role in Fighting Childhood Obesity

Michelle Murphy Zive

Parents should play a central role in preventing childhood obesity, argues Michelle Murphy Zive in the following viewpoint. They can start by maintaining a healthy weight themselves, she explains, which will reduce the chance that they will have an obese child. In addition, adds Zive, parents should encourage their children to consume healthy foods and smaller portions, and to engage in physical activity. Zive is a registered dietitian with over fifteen years of experience working with schools in improving students' health.

As you read, consider the following questions:
1. In the author's opinion, what role does genetics play in childhood obesity?
2. According to Zive, how does a baby show that it is tuned in to its hunger-satiety mechanism?
3. Why does the author suggest giving infants vegetables and meat before sweet fruits?

Michelle Murphy Zive, "Childhood Obesity: What Parents Can Do," www.nutritionnetworknews.org, 2004. Copyright © 2004 by Nutrition Network News. Reproduced by permission.

You've probably heard the statistics. Childhood obesity has doubled over the last 20 years, affecting 10 million children. One in five children are either overweight or obese. Diseases once thought of as adult onset, including obesity, are now affecting children. For instance, with the obesity epidemic, there has been an alarming increase in Type 2 diabetes. Not only does obesity affect our children physically, but there is a negative impact on them socially and emotionally.

True or false? As parents, there's nothing you can do to prevent obesity, since it's based on genetics. Absolutely false. Yes, there is a propensity for overweight parents to have overweight kids. But the shocking increase in obesity has little to do with genetics and is influenced mainly by the environment, including the home.

Simply put, children are eating more calories than they are expending. The rise in the number of hours children sit in front of the television or computer, the increase in soda consumption, the lack of structured physical education in schools have all contributed to the obesity epidemic.

One day there may be a way to manipulate genes in order to prevent such diseases as obesity, but for right now the key to preventing obesity is to change the environment where a child is more likely to eat less calories and be more physically active.

The California Health and Human Services, Primary Care and Family Health Division and the University of California Berkeley–Center for Weight and Health hosted the 2003 California Childhood Obesity Conference in San Diego. The conference entitled, "Making an Impact Now: Environmental, Family and Clinical Approaches," focused on solving the childhood/adolescent obesity epidemic. Below are just some of the suggestions parents can follow to impact or prevent obesity and ensure their children are the healthiest they can possibly be. After all, a child learns what food to like, what to eat, when to eat, food rules and how much to eat in their environment which is largely 'controlled' by parents.

In the Womb

The health of a baby starts in the womb. Staying away from cigarettes, alcohol and drugs, and eating right with lots of fruits and vegetables while pregnant ensures the health of the baby (and the mother). The same is true for watching your weight while you're pregnant. The current recommendation is to gain between 25–35 pounds while pregnant. Beyond this, complications with the baby and mother, including having a large baby, can happen. There are studies that show a large baby can lead to a large child and then to a large adult. In fact, 80% of obese children become obese adults.

If you're diagnosed with gestational diabetes (the diabetes you get when you're pregnant), then it's important to follow the diabetic diet prescribed by your doctor in order to control your blood sugar. This usually includes lean protein (like chicken and lean beef), fruits and vegetables, whole grains, and low fat dairy. If your blood sugar is not controlled, then the 'extra' sugar in the blood passes from you to the baby and increases the likelihood that you will have a big baby. Get plenty of physical activity as well (with or without gestational diabetes), this will help with lowering your blood sugar and keeping your weight in check.

Infancy

Breastfeeding is the best way to prevent over fatness in babies compared to bottle-feeding. Breast milk contains the perfect amount of calories, fat, and vitamins and minerals for proper growth of the baby. Furthermore, fat levels in breast milk increase as a child feeds so that a child feels full after a limited amount of time. This is not true of bottle-feeding, where more often than not the parent feeds the 'entire' bottle to the infant. Also a breastfeeding mother learns cues from her baby, like turning her head away, when she's done. Proving at even this young age, a baby is in tune with their hunger-satiety mechanism.

At birth we favor sweet and salty tastes. Infants tend to reject sour or bitter tastes. Here in the US, we have a tendency to introduce fruits as an infant's first solid food. In Europe, parents are likely to introduce meat and vegetables as the first foods. If we were to give infants meat and vegetables first, there may be a better chance of infants learning to like and perhaps prefer these over sweet fruits. The key to food acceptance in infancy and throughout a child's life is repeated ex-

The Key Role of Parents

Betsy A. Keller, an associate professor of exercise and sport sciences at Ithaca College in New York, recently surveyed 130 parents about their children's weight and lifestyle.

She found that half of the parents of overweight children underestimated their child's weight status, deeming them at a normal weight. Keller said her study also found that parents misjudge how much exercise their children get.

"I don't think we're going to get at this issue of obesity until we ask the hard questions: What are you feeding your kid? What are you putting on the table? Why are you not doing some kind of physical activity with your kids?" she said.

Associated Press, http://msnbc.msn.com, July 6, 2004.

---

posure. Children are born neophobic, not liking new foods. Don't give up after a couple of times. Expose your infant to the 'disliked' food until it is accepted.

Toddler to Early Childhood

Like infants, toddlers and young children listen to their inner voice that tells them they are hungry or full. However, children are also beginning to look to their parents as role models. It is critical that parents model and practice those eating habits that they want their children to learn, such as liking fruits and vegetables, snacking only when hungry and making a conscious effort to eat low fat, low caloric food, like part-skim mozzarella cheese, chicken breast, and water.

Young children are natural grazers. Parents should keep cut up fruit and vegetables accessible and left out on a short table so children can snack on these items. Never force a child to finish the food on their plate.

Other parenting skills that should be used to encourage healthy eating and physical activity include:

- Find reasons to praise a child's behavior. There is good and bad behavior, not good and bad children. Focus on the child's behavior not the child.
- Never use food as a reward or punishment.
- Eat as many meals and snacks together as a family.
- Parents and caregivers should decide what to feed a child and when, but a child should determine whether to eat.

- Offer only healthy options. Allow a child to choose between healthy snacks like air-popped popcorn or an apple. Children want the chance to choose and choosing between healthy snacks is a win-win situation.
- Remove temptations. As parents you have the ability to purchase high-fat, high-sugar foods or not.
- Be consistent. Don't 'give in' when trying to do the right thing like teaching your children to eat right.
- Never force a child to eat or not eat. Research shows that if you allow a child to determine what they eat, they are more likely to eat healthy and not overeat. Set limits and allow your child to choose within those limits.
- Let your children play. At this age, they love to play and learn that 'physical activity' can be fun!

Childhood to Teens

As a child grows, they begin to 'pull' away from their parents. But not all is lost. Parents still have an enormous amount of influence on their children in the home.

- Have bowls of washed cut up fruit and vegetables available.
- Limit the amount of time spent in front of the television and computer. Because overeating in front of these is likely, only eat at the table.
- Drive your child to sports practices.
- Limit the amount of food you serve your child. Try using smaller plates.
- Do have lots of cold water, 1% or nonfat milk, or 100% fruit juice instead of soda available.
- When dining out, choose restaurants that have healthy choices.

Periodical Bibliography

The following articles have been selected to supplement the diverse views presented in this chapter.

Daniel Akst	"Shedding Pounds with Medicare," *New York Times*, July 25, 2004.
Radley Balko	"Before Feds Invade Your Kitchen, Anti-Fat Funding Should Be Voted On," *Los Angeles Times*, July 30, 2004.
Radley Balko, Kelly Brownell, and Marion Nestle	"Are You Responsible for Your Own Weight?" *Time*, June 7, 2004.
Doug Bandow	"Advocates Declare War on Obesity—and Us," *Conservative Chronicle*, September 29, 2004.
Philip Elmer-De Witt	"The New Battle of the Bulge," *Time*, June 7, 2004.
Jeffrey M. Friedman	"A War on Obesity, Not the Obese," *Science*, February 7, 2003.
Nick Gillespie	"American Slender: When Did Freedom Become Just Another Word for 10 Pounds Left to Lose?" *Reason*, August/September 2004.
Emily Heil	"Can Big Government Fight Big Waistlines?" *National Journal*, October 18, 2003.
Issues and Controversies On File	"Obesity," April 9, 2004.
Tania Kindersley	"A Job for Many," *Spectator*, July 6, 2002.
New Statesman	"How to Cut Obesity," May 31, 2004.
Science	"The Ironic Politics of Obesity," February 7, 2003.
Walter Williams	"Is This the America We Want?" *Conservative Chronicle*, June 18, 2003.

For Further Discussion

Chapter 1

1. The authors in chapter one present various opinions on the extent of obesity in the United States and around the world. Based on your reading of these viewpoints, do you believe obesity is a serious problem? Back up your answer with statistics and examples from the viewpoints.

2. After reading the viewpoints about worldwide obesity by the World Health Organization and Paul Campos, list the major pieces of evidence that the authors use to support their arguments. In your opinion, which of the two authors uses the most credible evidence? Explain.

3. The World Health Organization, Paul Campos, the U.S. Department of Health and Human Services, and Dan Mindus all discuss the usefulness of the body mass index (BMI) as a measure of obesity. After reading their viewpoints, do you believe the BMI is a good tool for analyzing a person's weight? Cite from the texts to back up your answer.

Chapter 2

1. Amanda Spake and Mary Brophy Marcus assert that overeating and lack of exercise cause obesity. Sandy Szwarc contends that this belief is incorrect. In your opinion, which of these authors makes the strongest argument about the cause of obesity? Why?

2. According to the American Obesity Association, obesity should be viewed as a disease. However, George Hawley argues that to classify obesity as a disease implies that the obese individual has no control over his or her weight, which Hawley believes is not true. After reading these two viewpoints, do you think obesity should be classified as a disease? Support your answer with specifics from the viewpoints.

3. What statistics does Michael D. Lemonick use to help support his contention that obesity is a result of human evolution? Which do you find most convincing? Least convincing?

Chapter 3

1. Nancy Naomi advocates gastric bypass surgery as a highly effective way for the obese to lose weight and become healthier. The *Religion & Society Report* contends that obesity can, and should, be reduced simply by eating less. Do you think gastric bypass surgery should be an easily available option for obese people? Why or

why not? Can you think of any cases in which the surgery might be a bad choice? Cite from the viewpoints to explain your answer.

2. Both Lester M. Crawford and Robert C. Atkins agree that the majority of the weight-loss drugs currently available either pose possible health risks or are not effective. However, these authors disagree on the role that weight-loss drugs might play in the fight against obesity. Do you believe drugs are a good solution for reducing obesity? Back up your answer with statistics and examples from the viewpoints.

3. According to John H. Banzhaf III, lawsuits against fast food restaurants are an effective way to reduce obesity. In opposition, Todd G. Buchholz argues that restaurants cannot be held responsible for what people decide to eat. After reading these viewpoints, make two lists: one outlining the potential advantages of lawsuits against the food industry, and another enumerating the potential harms of such lawsuits. After examining your lists, decide whether you think lawsuits against the food industry should be allowed. Explain your position, using evidence from your lists.

Chapter 4

1. The authors in chapter four offer a number of different arguments about who should take responsibility for the problems caused by obesity. After reading these viewpoints, who do you believe should be the first to take a role in fighting obesity and its resultant problems? Quote from the viewpoints to support your answer.

2. David Boaz believes that by blaming society for obesity, taxpayers will be unfairly forced to pay for the consequences of individual behavior. Morgan Downey disagrees. He argues that obesity, like diseases such as cancer, must be addressed by the community. In your opinion, what problems might result from treating obesity solely as a matter of individual responsibility? Might this policy have negative effects on people not suffering from obesity? Explain.

3. Ellen Ruppel Shell argues that the government should take action to reduce obesity. Robert E. Wright contends that government intervention will be ineffective. Examine the evidence offered by both authors and present your own opinion about whether the government should take responsibility for obesity.

4. Gerard J. Musante explains that obesity is due to individual choices, and the best way to reduce it is through education. Do you agree with his argument? Explain, citing from the viewpoint to support your answer.

Organizations to Contact

The editors have compiled the following list of organizations concerned with the issues debated in this book. The descriptions are derived from materials provided by the organizations. All have publications or information available for interested readers. The list was compiled on the date of publication of the present volume; names, addresses, phone and fax numbers, and e-mail addresses may change. Be aware that many organizations take several weeks or longer to respond to inquiries, so allow as much time as possible.

American Association of Diabetes Educators (AADE)
100 West Monroe, Fourth Floor, Chicago, IL 60603
(312) 424-2426 • fax: (312) 424-2427
e-mail: aade@aadenet.org • Web site: www.aadenet.org

AADE is a multidisciplinary organization representing over ten thousand health care professionals whose goal is to advance the role of the diabetes educator and improve the quality of diabetes education and care. The association publishes the latest diabetes education research; its publications include *Diabetes Educator* and *AADE News*. On its Web site, the association provides a search engine to locate local diabetes educators, access to its research database, and links to related sites.

American Diabetes Association (ADA)
National Service Center
1701 North Beauregard St., Alexandria, VA 22311
(703) 549-1500 • fax: (703) 549-6996
e-mail: customerservice@diabetes.org
Web site: www.diabetes.org

The ADA is a nonprofit health organization providing diabetes research, information, and advocacy. The mission of the organization is to prevent and cure diabetes and to improve the lives of all people affected by diabetes. To fulfill this mission, ADA funds research, publishes scientific findings, and provides information and other services to people with diabetes, their families, health care professionals, and the public. It publishes many books and resources including the monthly *Diabetes Forecast*. On its Web site, the ADA provides news and information on type 1 and type 2 diabetes, a search engine to obtain local information, and access to some of its journal articles.

American Dietetic Association
120 S. Riverside Plaza, Suite 2000, Chicago, IL 60606
(312) 899-0040 • fax: (312) 899-1979
e-mail: adaf@eatright.org • Web site: www.eatright.org
The American Dietetic Association is the largest organization of
food and nutrition professionals in the United States. It works to
shape the food choices of the public for optimal nutrition, health,
and well-being. The association publishes the monthly *Journal of
the American Dietetic Association* as well as a variety of booklets,
pamphlets, and fact sheets about nutrition.

American Enterprise Institute (AEI)
1150 Seventeenth St. NW, Washington, DC 20036
(202) 862-5800 • fax: (202) 862-7178
Web site: www.aei.org
The American Enterprise Institute is dedicated to preserving and
strengthening the foundations of freedom through scholarly research, open debate, and publications. It believes that increased
government regulation is not the best way to reduce obesity. AEI
publishes dozens of reports on obesity, including "Obesity, Individual Responsibility, and Public Policy" and "It's a Family Affair."

American Medical Association (AMA)
515 N. State St., Chicago, IL 60610
(312) 464-5000
Web site: www.ama-assn.org
The AMA is the primary professional association of physicians in
the United States. Founded in 1847, it disseminates information to
its members and the public concerning medical breakthroughs,
medical and health legislation, and other issues concerning medicine
and health care, including obesity. The AMA operates a library and
offers many publications, including the weekly *JAMA: The Journal
of the American Medical Association* and the weekly newspaper *American Medical News*.

American Obesity Association (AOA)
1250 Twenty-Fourth St. NW, Suite 300, Washington, DC 20037
(202) 776-7711 • fax: (202) 776-7712
e-mail: pr@obesity.org • Web site: www.obesity.org
The goal of the American Obesity Association is to change public
policy and perceptions about obesity. It believes obesity is not just
a result of personal behavior but is a complex disease related to environment and genetic heritage. Its AOA Research Foundation

works to find a cure for obesity. The association publishes numerous reports, fact sheets, and charts about obesity.

American Public Health Association (APHA)
800 I St. NW, Washington, DC 20001
(202) 777-2742 • fax: (202) 777-2534
e-mail: comments@apha.org • Web site: www.apha.org

APHA works to protect and promote the public's health through education and prevention. It publishes numerous books, manuals, and pamphlets about obesity, including, "The Obesity Epidemic in U.S. Minority Communities" and "Toolkit for Childhood Obesity Intervention." The association also publishes the monthly *American Journal of Public Health* and the *Nation's Health*, which is published ten times per year.

Brookings Institution
1775 Massachusetts Ave. NW, Washington, DC 20036-2188
(202) 797-6105 • fax: (202) 797-2495
e-mail: brookinfo@brookings.edu • Web site: www. brook.edu

The institution is a liberal research and education organization that publishes material on economics, government, and foreign policy. It strives to serve as a bridge between scholarship and public policy, bringing new knowledge to the attention of decision makers and providing scholars with insight into public policy issues. The Brookings Institution publishes numerous reports on obesity, including "All This Progress Is Killing Us, Bite by Bite" and "Health in the Age of Globalization."

Cato Institute
1000 Massachusetts Ave. NW, Washington, DC 20001-5403
(202) 842-0200 • fax: (202) 842-3490
e-mail: cato@cato.org • Web site: www.cato.org

The Cato Institute is a libertarian public policy research foundation dedicated to limiting the role of government and protecting individual liberties. The institute publishes the quarterly magazine *Regulation*, the bimonthly *Cato Policy Report*, and numerous commentaries on obesity, including "Obesity and Medicare" and "The 'War' Against Obesity."

The Heritage Foundation
214 Massachusetts Ave. NE, Washington, DC 20002
(202) 546-4400 • fax: (202) 546-8328
e-mail: info@heritage.org • Web site: www.heritage.org

The Heritage Foundation is a public policy research institute that supports limited government and the free market system. It is opposed to heavy government involvement in health care issues. The foundation publishes the quarterly *Policy Review* as well as a number of papers on the topic of obesity, including "Obesity and Life Styles: Is It the Hamburger or Your House?" "Sprawl and Obesity: A Flawed Connection," and "Today's Special: Another 'Hunger Crisis.'"

International Association for the Study of Obesity (IASO)
e-mail: enquiries@iaso.org • Web site: www.iaso.org

IASO is an international organization dedicated to promoting the understanding of obesity through scientific research and dialogue, and to encouraging the development of effective policies for obesity prevention and management. Its International Obesity Taskforce works with the World Health Organization to inform the world about the urgency of the obesity problem. IASO publishes a variety of information about obesity in the *International Journal of Obesity*, *Obesity Reviews*, and *Obesity Newsletter*, all available on its Web site.

Kaiser Family Foundation
2400 Sand Hill Rd., Menlo Park, CA 94025
(650) 854-9400 • fax: (650) 854-4800
Web site: www.kff.org

The Henry J. Kaiser Family Foundation is an independent philanthropy focusing on the major health issues facing the nation. The foundation is an independent voice and source of facts and analysis for policy makers, the media, the health care community, and the general public. The foundation contracts with a wide range of outside individuals and organizations through its programs and continues to make a small number of grants for unsolicited proposals each year. It has published numerous papers, articles, and reports on obesity, including research on child obesity.

National Association to Advance Fat Acceptance (NAAFA)
PO Box 188620, Sacramento, CA 95818
(916) 558-6880 • fax: (916) 558-6881
e-mail: mbnaafa@aol.com • Web site: www.naafa.org

NAAFA works through public education and activism to end weight-based discrimination and to improve the quality of life for overweight people. The association provides information about the disadvantages of weight-loss treatments and publishes the bimonthly *NAAFA Newsletter*.

National Diabetes Alliance
4050 N. Maiden Dr., Baton Rouge, LA 70809
(225) 927-0317 • fax: (225) 928-0540
e-mail: mail@diabetesalliance.org
Web site: http://diabetesalliance.org
The mission of the alliance is to assist independent and allied diabetes organizations to improve the physical and social well-being of persons with diabetes. It is not a centralized agency but coordinates a project-by-project partnership of independent diabetes organizations with access to unified diabetes projects while maintaining their independent local governance. The alliance publishes an online magazine, *Diabetes America.*

National Institutes of Health (NIH)
(301) 496-4000
e-mail: nihinfo@od.nih.gov • Web site: www.nih.gov
The mission of the NIH is to discover new knowledge that will improve everyone's health. In order to achieve this mission, the NIH conducts and supports research, helps train research investigators, and fosters the communication of medical information. It publishes online fact sheets, brochures, and handbooks with information about obesity.

World Health Organization (WHO)
Web site: www.who.int
The World Health Organization is the United Nations' specialized agency for health. WHO's objective, as set out in its constitution, is the attainment by all peoples of the highest possible level of health. The organization believes that obesity poses a serious threat to health levels, and it aims to reduce obesity levels worldwide. Its Web site contains reports and fact sheets about obesity.

Bibliography of Books

Ben Agger — *Speeding Up Fast Capitalism: Cultures, Jobs, Families, Schools, Bodies.* Boulder, CO: Paradigm, 2004.

Sandra Alters — *Essential Concepts for Healthy Living.* Boston: Jones & Bartlett, 2003.

Claude Bouchard, ed. — *Physical Activity and Obesity.* Champaign, IL: Human Kinetics, 2000.

Walter Burniat, ed. — *Child and Adolescent Obesity: Causes, Consequences, Prevention, and Management.* New York: Cambridge University Press, 2002.

Joel Cohen — *Overweight Kids: Why Should We Care?* Sacramento: California Research Bureau, 2000.

Greg Critser — *Fat Land: How Americans Became the Fattest People in the World.* Boston: Houghton Mifflin, 2003.

Sharron Dalton — *Our Overweight Children: What Parents, Schools, and Communities Can Do to Control the Fatness Epidemic.* Berkeley: University of California Press, 2004.

Christopher G. Fairburn, ed. — *Eating Disorders and Obesity.* New York: Guilford, 2002.

Steven R. Feikin and Liz Zozanello Emery — *The Complete Book of Diet Drugs: Everything You Need to Know About Today's Prescription and Over-the-Counter Weight Loss Products.* New York: Kensington, 2000.

Glenn A. Gaesser and Steven N. Blair — *Big Fat Lies: The Truth About Your Weight and Health.* Carlsbad, CA: Gurze, 2002.

Gary Gardner, Brian Halweil, and Jane A. Peterson, eds. — *Underfed and Overfed: The Global Epidemic of Malnutrition.* Washington, DC: Worldwatch Institute, 2000.

Eve Gehling — *The Family and Friends' Guide to Diabetes: Everything You Need to Know.* New York: Wiley, 2000.

Bob Greene — *Get with the Program! Guide to Good Eating: Great Food for Health.* New York: Simon & Schuster, 2003.

Barry Gumbiner, ed. — *Obesity.* Philadelphia: American College of Physicians, 2001.

Edward J. Jackowski — *Escape Your Shape: How to Work Out Smarter, Not Harder.* New York: Simon & Schuster, 2001.

Joe L. Kincheloe — *The Sign of the Burger: McDonald's and the Culture of Power.* Philadelphia: Temple University Press, 2002.

R. Klettke — *A Guy's Gotta Eat: The Regular Guy's Guide to Eating Smart.* New York: Marlowe, 2003.

Gina Mallet — *Last Chance to Eat: The Fate of Taste in a Fast Food World.* New York: W.W. Norton, 2004.

J. Pervis Milnor III, Gregory L. Little, and Kenneth D. Robinson — *It Can Break Your Heart: What You and Your Doctor Should Know About Solving Your Weight Problem.* Memphis, TN: Eagle Wing, 2000.

Marion Nestle — *Food Politics: How the Food Industry Influences Nutrition and Health.* Berkeley: University of California Press, 2002.

Mimi Nichter — *Fat Talk: What Girls and Their Parents Say About Dieting.* Cambridge, MA: Harvard University Press, 2000.

Carol Emery Normadi and Laurelee Roark — *It's Not About Food: Change Your Mind, Change Your Life, End Your Obsession with Food and Weight.* New York: Berkley, 1999.

Linda O'Neill — *Having Diabetes.* Vero Beach, FL: Rourke, 2001.

Robert Poole — *Fat: Fighting the Obesity Epidemic.* New York: Oxford University Press, 2001.

George Ritzer — *The McDonaldization of Society.* Thousand Oaks, CA: Pine Forge, 2004.

Kendra Rosencrans — *Women Afraid to Eat: Breaking Free in Today's Weight-Obsessed Culture.* Hettinger, ND: Healthy Weight Network, 2000.

C. Ford Runge et al. — *Ending Hunger in Our Lifetime: Food Security and Globalization.* Baltimore: Johns Hopkins University Press, 2003.

Eric Schlosser — *Fast Food Nation: The Dark Side of the All-American Meal.* New York: HarperCollins, 2002.

Ellen Ruppel Shell — *The Hungry Gene: The Science of Fat and the Future of Thin.* New York: Atlantic Monthly, 2002.

Sondra Solovay — *Tipping the Scales of Justice: Fighting Weight-Based Discrimination.* Amherst, NY: Prometheus, 2000.

Jennifer Parker Talwar — *Fast Food, Fast Track: Immigrants, Big Business, and the American Dream.* Boulder, CO: Westview, 2002.

Kevin Thomson — *Handbook of Eating Disorders and Obesity.* Hoboken, NJ: John Wiley & Sons, 2004.

Pamela Walker

Understanding the Risks of Diet Drugs. New York: Rosen, 2000.

Gregory J. Welk and Steven N. Blair

Physical Activity Protects Against the Health Risks of Obesity. Washington, DC: President's Council on Physical Fitness and Sports, 2000.

Douglas Wetherill and Dean J. Kereiakes

Diabetes: What You Should Know. Cincinnati: Betterway, 2000.

Julian Whitaker

Reversing Diabetes. New York: Warner, 2001.

Index

198